SCHOLASTIC

Morning Jumpstarts: Math

100 Independent Practice Pages to Build Essential Skills

Marcia Miller & Martin Lee

New York · Toronto · London · Auckland · Sydney
Mexico City · New Delhi · Hong Kong · Buenos Aires

Teaching *Resources*

Edited by Mela Ottaiano
Cover design by Scott Davis
Interior design by Melinda Belter
Interior illustrations by Teresa Anderko, Melinda Belter, Maxie Chambliss, Steve Cox, Rusty Fletcher, James Graham Hale, and Mike Moran; © 2013 by Scholastic Inc.
ISBN: 978-0-545-46417-8

1 2 3 4 5 6 7 8 9 10   40   20 19 18 17 16 15 14 13

Contents

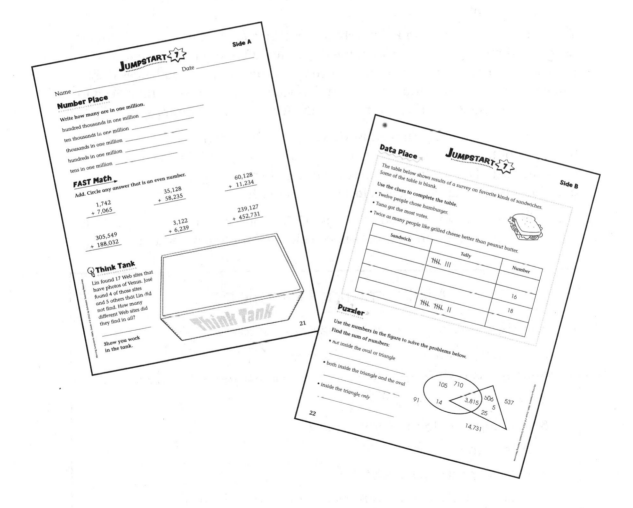

Introduction

In your busy classroom, you know how vital it is to energize students for the tasks of the day. That's why *Morning Jumpstarts: Math, Grade 4* is the perfect tool for you.

The activities in this book provide brief and focused individual practice in grade-level skills students are expected to master. Each Jumpstart is a two-page collection of five activities designed to review and reinforce a range of math skills and concepts students will build throughout the year. The consistent format helps students work independently and with confidence. Each Jumpstart includes these features:

- Number Place
- Data Place
- Fast Math
- Puzzler
- Think Tank

You can use a Jumpstart in its entirety or, because each feature is self-contained, assign sections at different times of the day or to different groups of learners. The Jumpstart activities will familiarize students with the kinds of challenges they will encounter on standardized tests, and provide a review of skills they need to master. (See page 6 for a close-up look at the features in each Jumpstart.)

The Common Core State Standards (CCSS) for Mathematics serve as the backbone of the activities in this book. On pages 7–8, you'll find a correlation chart that details how the 50 Jumpstarts dovetail with the widely accepted set of guidelines for preparing students to succeed in math.

Generally, we have kept in mind the eight CCSS "mathematical practices" that should inform solid math exploration, calculation, and interpretation.

Mathematical Practices

1. Make sense of problems and persevere in solving them.
2. Reason abstractly and quantitatively.
3. Construct viable arguments and critique the reasoning of others.
4. Model with mathematics.
5. Use appropriate tools strategically.
6. Attend to precision.
7. Look for and make use of structure.
8. Look for and express regularity in repeated reasoning.

Morning Jumpstarts: Math, Grade 4 © 2013 by Scholastic Teaching Resources

How to Use This Book

Morning Jumpstarts: Math, Grade 4 can be used in many ways—and not just in the morning! You know your students best, so feel free to pick and choose among the activities, and incorporate those as you see fit. You can make double-sided copies, or print one side at a time and staple the pages together.

We suggest the following times to present Jumpstarts:

- At the start of the school day, as a way to help students settle into the day's routines.
- Before lunch, as students ready themselves for their midday break.
- After lunch, as a calming transition into the afternoon's plans.
- Toward the end of the day, before students gather their belongings to go home, or as homework.

In general, the Jumpstarts progress in difficulty level and build on skills covered in previous sheets. Preview each one before you assign it to ensure that students have the skills needed to complete them. Keep in mind, however, that you may opt for some students to skip sections, as appropriate, or complete them together at a later time as part of a small-group or whole-class lesson.

Undoubtedly, students will complete Jumpstart activity pages at different rates. We suggest that you set up a "what to do when I'm done" plan to give students who need more time a chance to finish without interruption. For example, you might encourage students to complete another Jumpstart or get started on a math homework assignment.

An answer key begins on page 109. You might want to review answers with the whole class. This approach provides opportunities for discussion, comparison, extension, reinforcement, and correlation to other skills and lessons in your current plans. Your observations can direct the kinds of review or reinforcement you may want to add to your lessons. Alternatively, you may find that having students discuss activity solutions and strategies in small groups is another effective approach.

When you introduce the first Jumpstart, walk through its features with your class to provide an overview before you assign it and to make sure students understand the directions. Help students see that the activities in each section focus on different kinds of skills, and let them know that the same sections will repeat throughout each Jumpstart, always in the same order and position. You might want to work through the first few Jumpstarts as a group until students are comfortable with the routine and ready to work independently.

You know best how to assign the work to the students in your class. You might, for instance, stretch a Jumpstart over two days, assigning Side A on the first day and Side B on the second. Although the activities on different Jumpstarts vary in difficulty and in time needed, we anticipate that once students are familiar with the routine, most will be able to complete both sides of a Jumpstart in anywhere from 10 to 20 minutes.

A Look Inside

Each two-page Jumpstart includes the following skill-building features.

Number Place The first feature on Side A reviews grade-appropriate place-value skills related to whole numbers, decimals, and fractions. Regardless of the particular presentation, students will use their knowledge of place value and their number sense to complete this feature. A solid place-value foundation is essential for success with computation and estimation, and for an overall grasp of numerical patterns and relationships.

Fast Math The second Side A feature addresses necessary grade-level computation skills with the goal of building automaticity, fluency, and accuracy. To work through these exercises, students draw upon their understanding of computation strategies and mathematical properties. In some instances, students will review skills that have been covered previously. This is a good way to keep math skills sharp and to point out to you where revisiting a skill or algorithm may be beneficial.

Think Tank This feature rounds out Side A by offering an original word problem that draws from a wide spectrum of grade-appropriate skills, strategies, and approaches. Some are single-step problems; others require multiple steps to solve. The think tank itself provides a place where students can draw, do computations, and work out their thinking. This is a particularly good section to discuss together, to share solutions, as well as to compare and contrast approaches and strategies. Encourage students to recognize that many problems can be solved in more than one way, or may have more than one solution.

Data Place Every Side B begins with an activity in which students solve problems based on reading, collecting, representing, and interpreting data that is presented in many formats: lists, tables, charts, pictures, and, mostly, in a variety of graphs. In our rapidly changing world, it is essential that students build visual literacy by becoming familiar with many kinds of graphic presentations. This feature presents the kinds of graphs students are likely to encounter online, on TV, and in newspapers and magazines. Some include data from other curriculum areas.

Puzzler Side B always ends with an entertaining challenge: a brainteaser, puzzle, non-routine problem, code, or other engaging task designed to stretch the mind. While some students may find this section particularly challenging, others will relish teasing out trick solutions. This feature provides another chance for group work or discussion. It may prove useful to have pairs of students tackle these together. And, when appropriate, invite students to create their own challenges, using ideas sparked by these exercises. Feel free to create your own variations of any brainteasers your class enjoys.

Morning Jumpstarts: Math, Grade 4 © 2013 by Scholastic Teaching Resources

Connections to the Common Core State Standards

As shown in the chart below and on page 8, the activities in this book will help you meet your specific state math standards as well as those outlined in the CCSS. These materials address the following standards for students in grade 4. For details on these standards, visit the CCSS Web site: www.corestandards.org/the-standards/.

JS	Operations & Algebraic Thinking					Number & Operations in Base Ten						Number & Operations —Fractions							Measurement & Data						Geometry		
	4.OA.1	4.OA.2	4.OA.3	4.OA.4	4.OA.5	4.NBT.1	4.NBT.2	4.NBT.3	4.NBT.4	4.NBT.5	4.NBT.6	4.NF.1	4.NF.2	4.NF.3	4.NF.4	4.NF.5	4.NF.6	4.NF.7	4.MD.1	4.MD.2	4.MD.3	4.MD.4	4.MD.5	4.MD.7	4.G.1	4.G.2	4.G.3
1			•	•	•		•		•													•					
2	•	•	•		•		•		•											•		•	•				
3	•	•	•				•													•		•					
4		•	•		•		•		•													•					
5			•		•	•	•		•													•					
6			•	•	•	•	•	•	•	•										•	•	•			•		
7	•		•	•		•	•		•													•					
8			•		•		•	•	•													•			•	•	
9	•	•	•		•				•	•	•				•							•			•		
10			•				•		•											•		•					
11	•	•	•		•		•		•	•	•											•					
12	•	•	•	•	•	•	•		•		•				•							•					
13			•		•			•	•											•		•					
14			•		•			•	•	•									•	•	•	•			•	•	
15	•	•	•		•			•	•										•	•		•					
16			•	•	•		•		•											•		•					
17	•		•				•		•	•									•	•	•	•			•		
18	•		•		•	•	•	•	•								•			•		•	•		•		
19	•	•	•	•	•	•			•	•	•								•	•		•					
20	•	•	•	•	•	•			•	•									•	•	•	•					
21	•	•	•			•	•		•													•					
22	•	•	•			•	•	•	•											•		•					
23	•	•	•			•	•	•	•													•					
24	•	•	•		•				•	•	•	•	•							•		•					
25	•	•	•			•	•		•	•											•		•		•	•	

JS	4.OA.1	4.OA.2	4.OA.3	4.OA.4	4.OA.5	4.NBT.1	4.NBT.2	4.NBT.3	4.NBT.4	4.NBT.5	4.NBT.6	4.NF.1	4.NF.2	4.NF.3	4.NF.4	4.NF.5	4.NF.6	4.NF.7	4.MD.1	4.MD.2	4.MD.3	4.MD.4	4.MD.5	4.MD.7	4.G.1	4.G.2	4.G.3
26	•	•	•		•	•	•	•	•	•												•			•	•	
27	•	•	•						•	•	•						•			•		•					
28	•	•	•	•							•						•			•		•					
29	•	•	•		•				•		•							•		•		•					
30	•				•	•				•	•				•		•	•				•					
31	•		•		•	•	•			•	•						•	•	•	•		•					
32	•	•	•		•		•	•		•	•				•		•	•		•		•					•
33			•		•		•	•	•	•	•						•	•	•			•				•	
34	•	•	•		•			•	•	•	•					•	•	•	•	•		•					
35		•	•		•				•	•	•			•			•	•		•		•					
36	•	•	•		•				•	•	•						•	•	•	•		•					
37		•	•		•		•		•		•				•		•			•		•					
38			•		•				•			•	•				•	•		•		•					
39		•	•		•	•			•					•		•	•	•	•	•		•	•		•	•	
40	•	•			•			•	•	•				•			•	•	•			•					
41	•	•			•			•	•	•	•	•	•	•			•		•	•		•					
42			•	•	•				•						•		•	•		•		•				•	
43	•	•			•				•	•					•	•	•		•			•	•				
44	•	•	•		•					•	•			•			•					•	•				
45	•	•	•		•		•							•	•		•					•			•	•	
46			•							•		•		•			•			•		•					
47	•								•	•	•			•			•		•			•					
48		•						•									•			•		•			•	•	
49		•								•	•						•			•		•	•	•	•		
50	•		•		•					•				•								•	•			•	•

Morning Jumpstarts: Math, Grade 4 © 2013 by Scholastic Teaching Resources

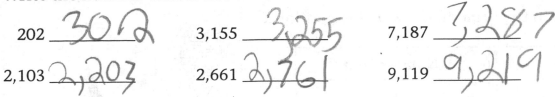
Name _Elliott_   Date _____

Number Place

Write the number that is **100** *more*.

202 __302__   3,155 __3,255__   7,187 __3,287__

2,103 __2,203__   2,661 __2,761__   9,119 __9,219__

Write the number that is **100** *less*.

323 __223__   2,379 __2,279__   2,296 __2,196__

834 __734__   5,405 __5,305__   5,140 __5,040__

FAST Math

Add. Circle the greatest sum.

4 + 7 = __11__   9 + 6 = __15__   8 + 7 = __15__

3 + 9 = __12__   6 + 9 = __15__   8 + 3 = __11__

7 + 9 = __16__   8 + 9 = __17__   9 + 9 = (__18__)

Think Tank

Ken has fewer absences than Meg, but more than Dan. Ming has been absent more than Meg. Who has been absent the most?

__Ming__

Show your work in the tank.

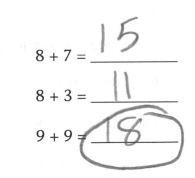

M M K D

Think Tank

+2
+31
+17
+24
+60
151

Data Place

The table shows some different sports equipment sold at a sporting goods store one week.

Use the data in the table to answer the questions.

Item	Number Sold
Baseball Glove	19
Soccer Ball	31
Tennis Racquet	17
Hockey Stick	24
Swimsuit	60

1. How many hockey sticks were sold? _____24_____

2. How many of the sports items were sold in all? _____151_____

3. Which item sold about three times as much as the baseball glove did?
_____Soccer Ball_____

Puzzler

Count *on* by 11 to connect the dots.

Hint: There are six numbers not used.

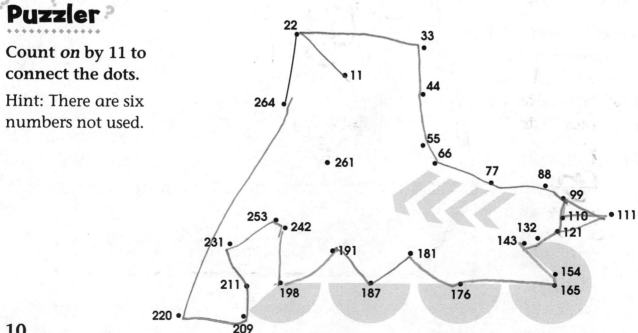

10

Morning Jumpstarts: Math, Grade 4 © 2013 by Scholastic Teaching Resources

Side A

Name _____ Date _____

Number Place

Write the place value of the underlined digit.

4,5<u>6</u>7 _____ 60

9,<u>3</u>56 _____ 300

<u>4</u>4,212 _____ 40,000

<u>1</u>,849 _____ 1,000

21<u>2</u>,873 _____ 10,000

12,<u>2</u>80 _____ 2000

<u>9</u>3,518 _____ 90,000

82,<u>6</u>94 _____ 600

7,4<u>6</u>1 _____ 60

<u>1</u>01,605 _____ 100,000

FAST Math

Subtract. Circle any answer that is your age.

14 – 4 = 10

17 – 8 = 9

12 – 6 = 6

16 – 9 = 7

18 – 5 = 13

18 – 10 = 8

18 – 9 = 9

15 – 7 = 8

17 – 7 = 10

Think Tank

Jin has $20. She bought flowers for $3.50 and a gift for $2 more than that. She bought a card for $1.95. How much did she spend in all?

7.45

Show your work in the tank.

Morning Jumpstarts: Math, Grade 4 © 2013 by Scholastic Teaching Resources

11

Data Place

Use the circle graph about singers in the school chorus to answer the questions.

School Chorus

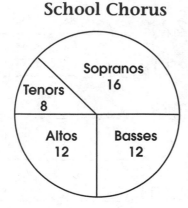

Tenors 8
Sopranos 16
Altos 12
Basses 12

1. How many singers are in the chorus? ___48___

2. How many basses are in the chorus? ___12___

3. Which sections of the chorus have the same number of members?

___Altos , Basses___

4. Which section has twice the number of members as the tenor section does?

___Sopranos___

Puzzler

A magic square is an ancient math puzzle. The Chinese first made the puzzle over 2,600 years ago.

The numbers from 1–9 appear only *once* each in the 9 boxes of the square. The sum of each row, column, and diagonal must be 15. Three of the numbers are already in place. Figure out which numbers go in the other boxes.

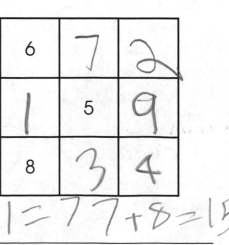

6	7	2
1	5	9
8	3	4

Explain your solution method.

$6+7=13$ $13+2=15$ $6+1=7$ $7+8=15$

$6+5=11$ $11+4=15$ $4+3=7$ $7+8=15$

12

Morning Jumpstarts: Math, Grade 4 © 2013 by Scholastic Teaching Resources

Name _____ Date _____

Number Place

Write each number in standard form.

three thousand fifteen ___3,015___

twenty-nine thousand four hundred thirty-seven ___29,437___

six hundred forty-three thousand ___643,000___

eighty-two thousand three hundred eleven ___82,3011___

FAST Math

Add. Circle any answer that is an odd number.

+1 17 + 48	+1 29 + 29	+1 38 + 58	+1 125 + 345	+1 134 + 656	+1 417 + 417
65	58	96	470	780	834

Think Tank

Lisa has a package that costs $3.95 to mail. She pays with 3 dollar bills and 4 quarters. How much change should Lisa get back?

___5¢___

Show your work in the tank.

Data Place

Use the graph about trail lengths to answer the questions.

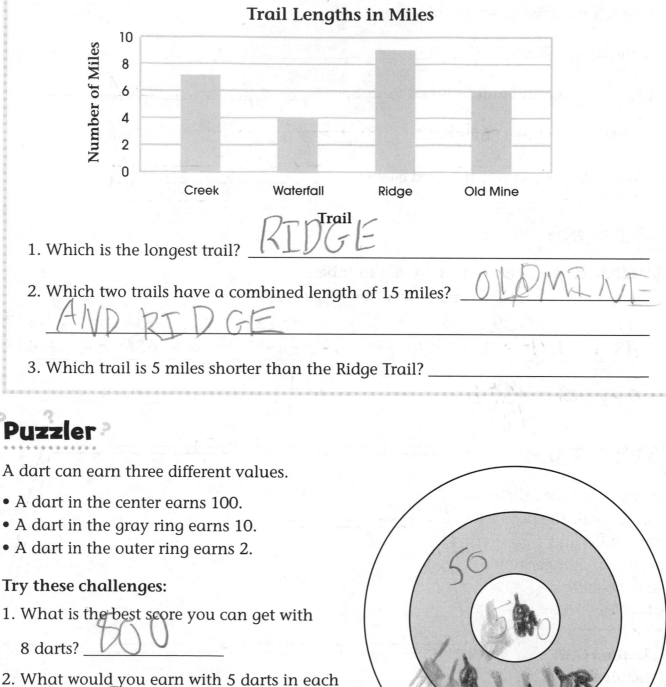

Trail Lengths in Miles

1. Which is the longest trail? _RIDGE_

2. Which two trails have a combined length of 15 miles? _OLD MINE AND RIDGE_

3. Which trail is 5 miles shorter than the Ridge Trail? _____

Puzzler

A dart can earn three different values.

- A dart in the center earns 100.
- A dart in the gray ring earns 10.
- A dart in the outer ring earns 2.

Try these challenges:

1. What is the best score you can get with 8 darts? _800_

2. What would you earn with 5 darts in each section? _560_

3. Draw 5 red darts to make a score of 132.

4. Draw 10 blue darts to make a score of 150.

Name _____ Date _____

Number Place

Write each number in word form.

4,319 ___FOUR THOUSAND THRE HUNDRED___

44,159 ___FORTY FOUR THOUSAND ONE HUNDRED NINE TEEN___

27,008 ___TWENTY SEVEN THOUSAND ONE HUNDRED FIFTY NINE EIGHT___

60,006 ___SIXTY THOUSAND SIX___

309,254 ___THIRTY NINE THOUSAND TWO HUNDRED FIFTY FOUR___

FAST Math

Add. Find the sum of the greatest and least answers.

3,016 + 4,410 = __7,426__   140 + 807 = __1,207__   249 + 370 = __619__

1,209 + 7,005 = __7,214__   4,254 + 1,709 = __4,363__   156 + 918 = __1,074__

__7,426__ + __619__ = __8,045__

Think Tank

Alex, Ben, Cindy, and
Dee are in line for a movie.
Alex is third in line.
Dee is ahead of Cindy,
but behind Ben. Who is
first in line?

___BEN___

Show your work
in the tank.

B D A C

Morning Jumpstarts: Math, Grade 4 © 2013 by Scholastic Teaching Resources

Side B

Data Place

Greenleaf School voted on a school mascot.

Use the graph to answer the questions.

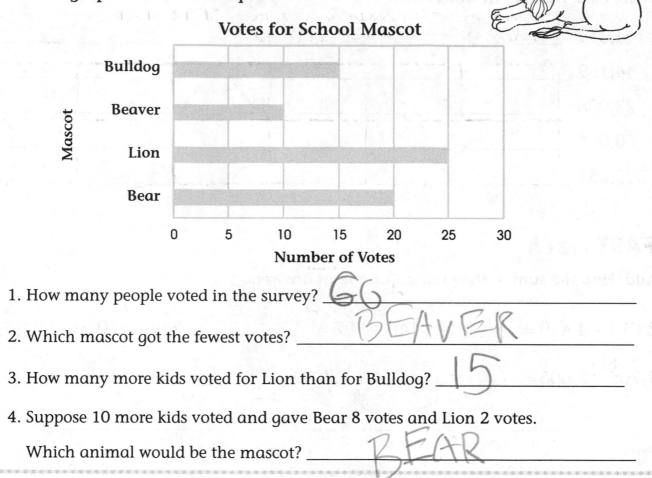

Votes for School Mascot

1. How many people voted in the survey? _____66_____

2. Which mascot got the fewest votes? _____BEAVER_____

3. How many more kids voted for Lion than for Bulldog? _____15_____

4. Suppose 10 more kids voted and gave Bear 8 votes and Lion 2 votes.

   Which animal would be the mascot? _____BEAR_____

Puzzler

Use the number with each pet to solve the number sentences below.

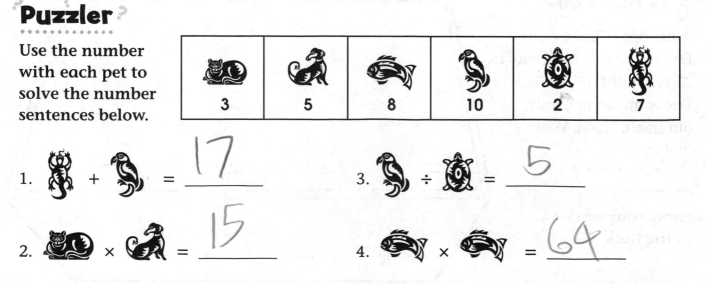

1. 🦎 + 🦜 = _____17_____

2. 🐱 × 🐕 = _____15_____

3. 🦜 ÷ 🐢 = _____5_____

4. 🐟 × 🐟 = _____64_____

16

Morning Jumpstarts: Math, Grade 4 © 2013 by Scholastic Teaching Resources

JUMPSTART 5

Name _____ Date _____

Number Place

Label the columns on the place value chart below from *Ones* to *Millions*.

Record the number that has *2 thousands, 8 hundreds, 5 ten-thousands, 0 hundred-thousands, 4 ones, 3 millions,* and *0 tens.*

54	O	800	200050000	300900		

FAST Math

Add. Circle any answer that is an even number.

```
    1,712          34,128          314
      421           2,218       31,004
  + 8,065         + 5,835           52
  -------         -------        +  666
   10,198          10,781         -------
                                  32,036
```

Think Tank

A scientist found 84 dinosaur eggs in one location and 201 in another location. She had expected to find 300 eggs. By how much did she miss her goal?

15

Show your work in the tank.

Think Tank

Data Place

Fourth graders took a survey about favorite kinds of movies.

Use the graph to answer the questions.

Movies We Like Best

Horror	🎟 🎟 🎟
Adventure	🎟 🎟
Comedy	🎟 🎟
Fantasy	🎟 🎟 🎟 🎟 🎟
Animated	🎟 🎟 🎟 🎟 🎟 🎟

Key 🎟 = 10 students

1. What does the key show? _____10_____

2. Which kind of movie do 15 students like best? ___COMEDY_____

3. Animated films got ___30_____ more votes than horror films.

4. How many students were surveyed? ___176_____

Puzzler

Solve the number puzzle. Use only the numbers 5, 6, 7, and 8 *once* inside every small square, and *once* in every row and column.

6	5	8	7
8	7	5	6
7	8	6	5
5	6	7	8

18

Morning Jumpstarts: Math, Grade 4 © 2013 by Scholastic Teaching Resources

Name _____ Date *July 4*

Number Place

Rewrite each number as only hundreds, only tens, or only ones.

Number	equals	Hundreds	or	Tens	or	Ones
300		3		30		300
600		~~600~~		60		6
1,800		8		0		1,800
2,700		27		0		2,700

FAST Math ▶

Add. Circle the sum closest to 500,000.

43,000 + 195,000 = 2,238   56,000 + 48,000 = 104,000

260,000 + 250,000 = 510,000   22,000 + 7,000 = 29,000

37,000 + 540,000 = 577,000   880,000 + 55,000 = 935,000

💡 Think Tank

Use the menu. Juan orders
3 burritos, 2 burgers,
4 sodas, and 1 juice.
He pays with a $20 bill.
What is his change?

3.89
_____

**Show your work
in the tank.**

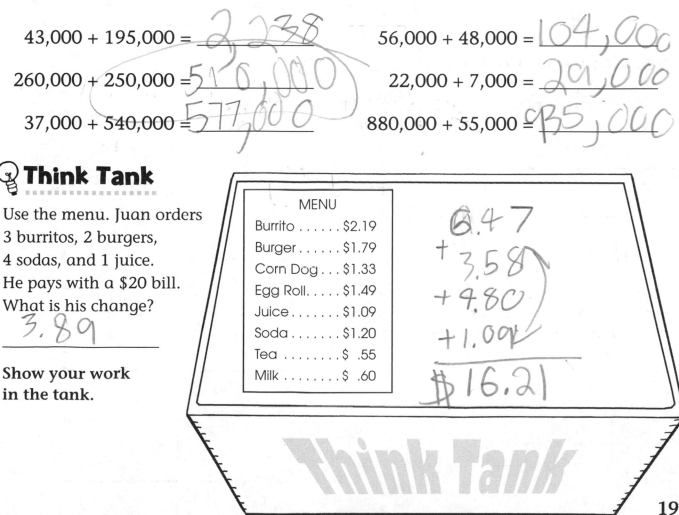

MENU
Burrito $2.19
Burger $1.79
Corn Dog . . . $1.33
Egg Roll. $1.49
Juice $1.09
Soda $1.20
Tea . . . . $ .55
Milk . . . . $ .60

6.47
+ 3.58
+ 4.80
+ 1.09
_____
$16.21

Think Tank

Data Place

A clothing store is taking a T-shirt inventory.

Complete the table to show all of the results.

T-Shirt Inventory

T-Shirt	Sizes			Total
	S	M	L	
Short Sleeve	27	35	42	104
Long Sleeve	36	18	21	75
V-Neck	49	9	31	89
Turtleneck	37	22	27	86
Sports Jersey	9	5	12	26

Puzzler

The shape below uses 5 squares and has a perimeter of 12 units.

Draw a shape that also uses 5 squares but has a perimeter of 10 units.

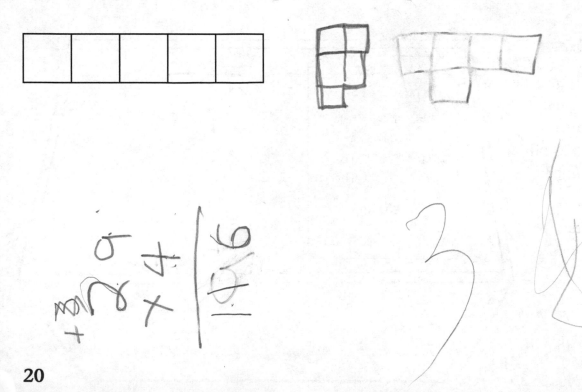

Morning Jumpstarts: Math, Grade 4 © 2013 by Scholastic Teaching Resources

Name _____ Date _____

Number Place

Write how many are in one million.

hundred-thousands in one million ___100___

ten-thousands in one million ___10,000___

thousands in one million ___1,000___

hundreds in one million ___10,000___

tens in one million ___100,000___

FAST Math

Add. Circle any answer that is an even number.

1,742	35,128	60,128
+ 7,065	+ 58,235	+ 11,234
8807	93763	71,362

305,549	3,122	239,127
+ 188,032	+ 6,239	+ 452,731
493581	9361	691858

Think Tank

Lin found 17 Web sites that have photos of Venus. José found 4 of those sites and 5 others that Lin did not find. How many different Web sites did they find in all?

___22___

Show you work in the tank.

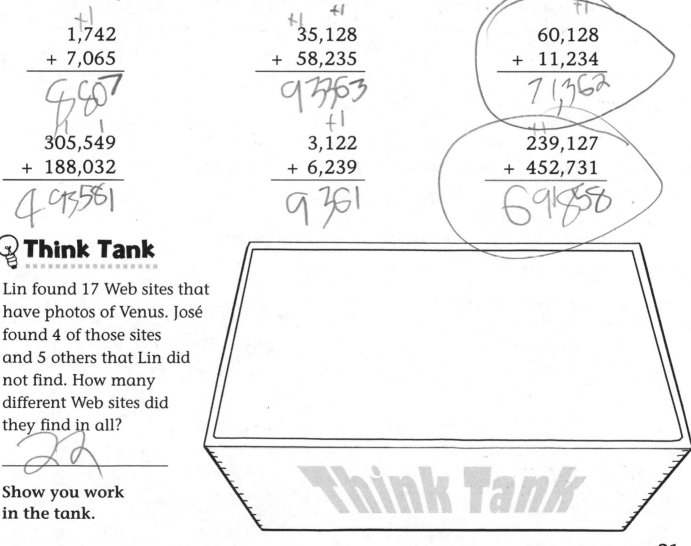

Data Place

The table below shows results of a survey on favorite kinds of sandwiches. Some of the table is blank.

Use the clues to complete the table.

• Twelve people chose hamburger.

• Tuna got the most votes.

• Twice as many people like grilled cheese better than peanut butter.

Sandwich	Tally	Number
Peanut butter	ΤΗΙ III	8
Grilled cheese	ΤΗΙ ΤΗΙ ΤΗΙ I	16
Tuna		18
Hamburger	ΤΗΙ ΤΗΙ II	12

Puzzler

Use the numbers in the figure to solve the problems below.

Find the sum of numbers:

• *not* inside the oval or triangle

91 14,731 537

• both inside the triangle and the oval

3,815

• inside the triangle *only*

5 506 25

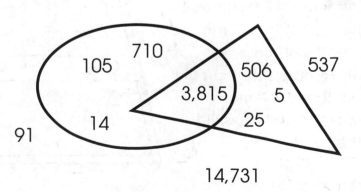

Morning Jumpstarts: Math, Grade 4 © 2013 by Scholastic Teaching Resources

Name _____ Date _____

Number Place

Write the number 1,000 *less*.

_59,000_ 60,000

_899,000_ 900,000

_999,000_ 1,000,000

Write the number 1,000 *more*.

2,399 _3,399_

54,799 _55,799_

999,000 _1,000,000_

FAST Math

Add. Circle the answer closest to one million.

```
     +1
  21,746
+  8,062
---------
  29,808
```

```
 +1  +1
  31,424
+ 88,935
---------
1 20,359
```

```
 +1 +1
  67,121
+ 19,284
---------
  86,405
```

```
 +1 +1
  360,040
+ 582,072
---------
  942,112
```

```
    +1
   3,122
+ 466,239
---------
     361
```

```
 +1 +1 +1
  939,183
+ 462,531
---------
1,401,714
```

Think Tank

Pete's Pizza offers 5 toppings and 4 kinds of crust. How many *different* pizzas could be made using 1 topping and 1 kind of crust?

_20_

Make a list or diagram the choices in the tank.

TOPPING	CRUST
Mushrooms	Regular
Onion	Thin
Pepperoni	Whole Wheat
Sausage	Very Thick
Extra Cheese	

Think Tank

Morning Jumpstarts: Math, Grade 4 © 2013 by Scholastic Teaching Resources

July 8

Data Place

Draw each point on the coordinate grid. Then connect the points in order to make a closed figure.

$(2, 1) \rightarrow (4, 3) \rightarrow (7, 3) \rightarrow (9, 1) \rightarrow (2, 1)$

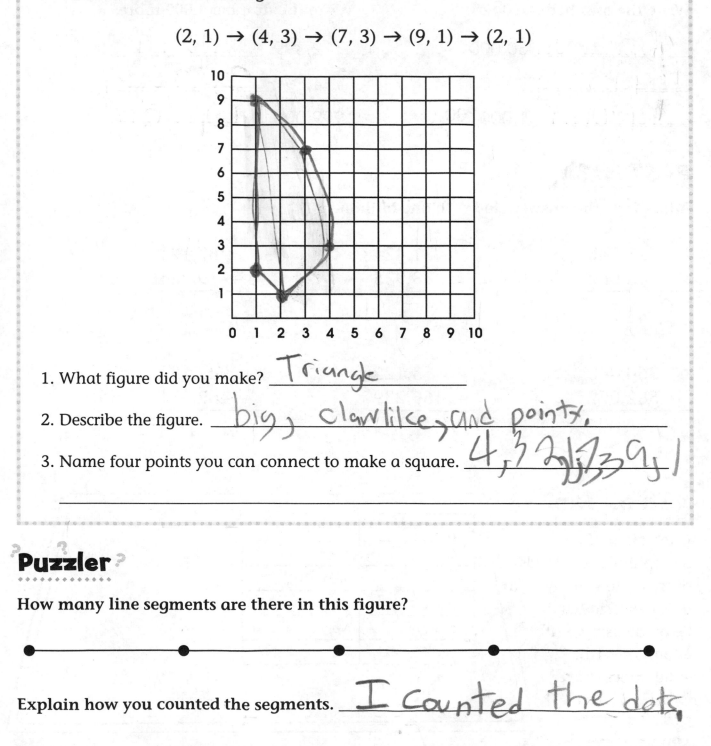

1. What figure did you make? __Triangle__

2. Describe the figure. __big, clawlike, and points.__

3. Name four points you can connect to make a square. __4,3 2,3 3 9,1__

Puzzler

How many line segments are there in this figure?

● ────── ● ────── ● ────── ● ────── ●

Explain how you counted the segments. __I counted the dots__

Morning Jumpstarts: Math, Grade 4 © 2013 by Scholastic Teaching Resources

Name _____ Date _____

Number Place

Write the number 10,000 *less.*

50,000   60,000

890,000   900,000

990,000   1,000,000

Write the number 100,000 *more.*

27,399   28,399

564,799   564,799

888,888   988,888

FAST Math

Subtract. Circle any answer whose digits add to less than 10.

```
  746          88          657
- 332        - 67        - 204
  414          21          453
```

```
  6,949        578         9,896
- 5,822      - 466       - 4,625
  1,127        114         5271
```

Think Tank

Saul's school is setting up chairs in the gym. Students have already set up 135 chairs. They will set up 320 in all. How many more chairs do they need to set up?

175

Show your work in the tank.

Think Tank

Data Place

The table shows the number of players in different sports leagues.

Use the data in the table to answer the questions.

Team	Players
Baseball	625
Soccer	420
Football	666
Hockey	222
Lacrosse	105

1. How many more players are in the football league than the baseball league?

   _39_

2. Which league has four times as many players as the lacrosse league has?

   Soccer

3. Which league has one-third as many players as the football league?

   Hockey

Puzzler

Trace over the design below without lifting your pencil or retracing any lines.

Try it first with your finger.

Then use a pencil or marker.

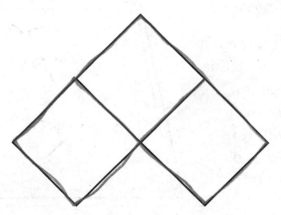

26

Morning Jumpstarts: Math, Grade 4 © 2013 by Scholastic Teaching Resources

Name _____   Date _____

Number Place

Compare. Write **<**, **=**, or **>**.

20,999 __<__ 29,000   15,551 __>__ 15,155

9,988 __<__ 10,000   90,404 __<__ 91,777

6,678 __<__ sixty-six thousand seventy-eight

forty-five thousand three hundred __=__ 45,300

FAST Math

Subtract. Circle any answer whose digits add to 10.

```
   5 14
  7,464          7 13          5 15
- 3,127          838          657
 4 3 5 7        - 657        - 294
                 181          363
```

```
   5 13          6 13           7 1
  6,345          5,738         9,816
- 5,812         - 4,266       - 7,425
  0 5 3 3        1 4 7 4       2 3 9 1
```

Think Tank

It is 139 miles from Phoenix, AZ, to Flagstaff, AZ. From there it is 79 more miles to the Grand Canyon. How far is it from Phoenix to the Grand Canyon?

218

Show your work in the tank.

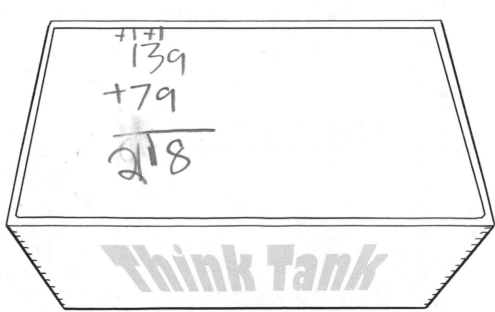

```
 1 1 1
  139
+ 79
  218
```

Morning Jumpstarts: Math, Grade 4 © 2013 by Scholastic Teaching Resources

Students were asked how many hours they spend each week using social media. The line plot shows the results.

Use the data in the line plot to answer the questions.

Hours Spent Using Social Media

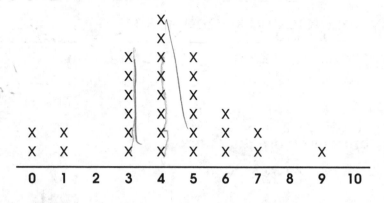

1. How many students were surveyed? _30_

2. What is the range of the data? _5_

3. What answer came up most often? _4_

4. How many students spend 5 hours each week using social media? _6_

5. How many students spend less than 5 hours each week using social media? _18_

Puzzler

Use each digit from 1–9 once only to form three addends whose sum is 999.

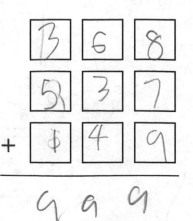

Morning Jumpstarts: Math, Grade 4 © 2013 by Scholastic Teaching Resources

Name _____ Date _____

Number Place

Order each set of numbers from *least* to *greatest*.

4,190   1,409   14,009   _1,409 4,190 14,009_

12,007   21,700   12,707   _12,003 12,707 21,700_

850,058   805,058   508,850   _508, 850 805,58 850,058_

21,000,000   12,200,000   210,200,000   _12,200,000 21,000,000 850,058_

FAST Math

Subtract. Circle any answer whose digits add to 15.

$$9,441 - 3,283 = 7,159$$

$$8,008 - 6,337 = 1,771$$

$$657 - 278 = 379$$

$$8,119 - 4,822 = 3,187$$

$$5\cancel{X}8 - 499 = 099$$

$$9,922 - 4,625 = 112$$

💡 Think Tank

Dodger Stadium in Los Angeles has 56,000 seats. The stadium in Florida where the Miami Marlins play has 36,331 seats. How many more seats are there in Dodger Stadium?

_19,668_

Show your work in the tank.

$$56,000 - 36,331 = 19,668$$

Data Place

Use the data in the calendar to answer the questions.

NOVEMBER

SUN	MON	TUE	WED	THU	FRI	SAT
		1	2	3	4	5
6	7	8	9	10	11	12
13	14	15	16	17	18	19
20	21	22	23	24	25	26
27	28	29	30			

1. Three dates in a row have a sum of 69. What are the dates?
   20, 24, 25

2. Two dates in a row have a product of 132. What are the dates?
   13 × 10 = 130

3. What is the product of dates on the 2nd and 3rd Sundays? 236

4. What is the quotient when you divide the date of the last Wednesday by the first Saturday? 6

Puzzler

Figure out each code. Fill in the blanket.

1. 3 × ♥ + ◀ = 11 and ◀ × △ = 10.

   If ♥ = 3, then ◀ = 2 and △ = 5.

2. 3 × ☺ − ☺ = ✳ and ✳ × 🎁 = 300.

   If 🎁 = 50, then ✳ = 300 and ☺ = 4.

Name _____ Date _____

Number Place

Rewrite each number as only hundreds, only tens, or only ones.

Number	equals	Hundreds	or	Tens	or	Ones
400		4		40		400
1,600		16		1600		1,600
9,000		90		900		9,000
24,000		240		2,400		24,000
410,000		410		41,000		410,000

FAST Math

Subtract. Circle any answer that is greater than 50,000.

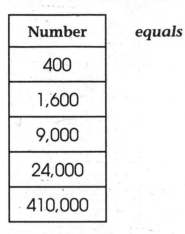

$$74,226 - 33,281 = 40945$$

$$8,038 - 697 = 7341$$

$$65,721 - 20,408 = 45312$$

$$69,249 - 5,872 = 63377$$

$$5,784 - 4,669 = 1115$$

$$90,896 - 2,628 = 88268$$

Think Tank

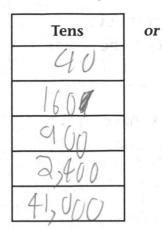
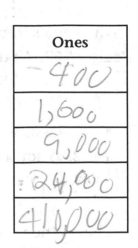

Jen is 26 years younger than her mom. Together, their ages total 50. How old is Jen?

8

How old is her mom?

26

Show your work in the tank.

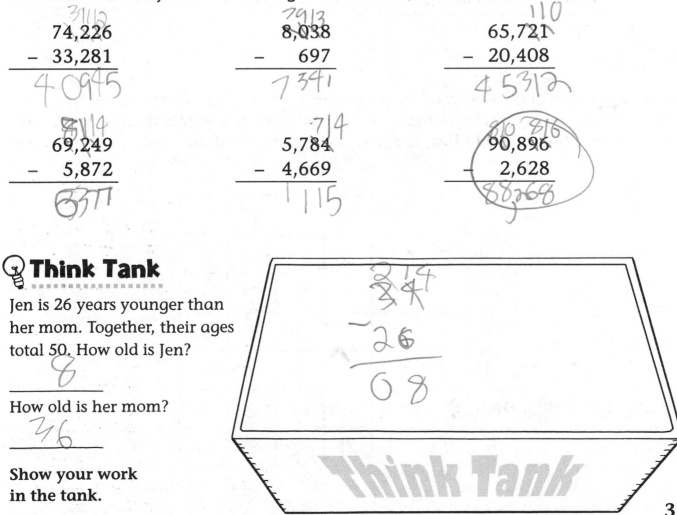

Morning Jumpstarts: Math, Grade 4 © 2013 by Scholastic Teaching Resources

Side B

+ P6
+ 1 6
+ 1 6
+ 1 6
+ 8

Data Place

Students in Mantle School voted for their favorite baseball teams. The results are shown in the table.

Use the data to answer the questions.

1. Which team got 3 times as many votes as the Tigers did? ___Rangers___

2. Which team got one-fourth as many votes as the Red Sox did? ___Marlins___

3. One team got 5 times the number of votes another got. Name the teams.
   ___Tigers   Redsox___

Mantle's Favorite Teams

Team	Votes
Dodgers	84
Yankees	56
Red Sox	88
Phillies	36
Tigers	16
Marlins	22
Rangers	48
Cardinals	80

Puzzler

Work your way through the math maze from *Start* to *Finish*. Alternate addition and subtraction sentences. Use a straight line to connect the three numbers in each sentence. The first two are already done.

START

24	47	71	86	14	37	22
101	59	7	105	96	11	26
12	23	89	9	93	72	66
69	5	116	37	20	36	55
81	25	56	87	73	122	27
60	75	123	45	80	44	70
8	138	35	21	17	43	117

FINISH

32

Morning Jumpstarts: Math, Grade 4 © 2013 by Scholastic Teaching Resources

Name _____ Date __July__ | Side A

Number Place

Round each number to the nearest ten *and* hundred.

Number	Nearest 10	Nearest 100
617	620	600
1,862	1,860	1,900
4,345	4,350	4,300
89,083	89,080	89,100

FAST Math

Estimate each sum by rounding.

7,226
+ 3,381
10000

8,938
+ 797
10000

68,727
+ 21,008
89,735
89,025

509,849
+ 311,372
822,231
820,231

5,724
+ 4,767
10,000

888,056
+ 32,148
910,204

Think Tank

Inez has five coins that total $.60. What are the coins?

3 Dimes 1 Quarter
1 Nickle

Show your work in the tank.

Data Place

Gracie and Will went to the SpaceFest. They got a schedule of events and talks at the Convention Center.

Use the schedule to answer the questions.

Event	Start	End
Meet & Greet	8:30 A.M.	9:15 A.M.
Space Stations	9:20 A.M.	10:25 A.M.
Alien Life	10:30 A.M.	11:25 A.M.
Satellites	11:30 A.M.	12:20 P.M.
Lunch	12:25 A.M.	1:25 P.M.
Astronaut Training	1:30 P.M.	2:25 P.M.
Space Vacations	2:30 P.M.	3:45 P.M.
Space Art	3:40 P.M.	5:00 P.M.

1. Which talk ends just before lunch?

   Satellites

2. Which talk lasts for 1 hour 15 minutes?

   Space Vacations

3. Which is the shortest talk?

   Meet and greet

4. Which is the longest talk? *Space art*

5. Which two talks last for the same amount of time? *Alien life, Astronauts training*

Puzzler

Each letter has a number value. Use the code to name an item that matches each of the descriptions below. Write the word and its value.

A = 1	B = 2	C = 3	D = 4	E = 5	F = 6	G = 7
H = 8	I = 9	J = 10	K = 11	L = 12	M = 13	N = 14
O = 15	P = 16	Q = 17	R = 18	S = 19	T = 20	U = 21
V = 22	W = 23	X = 24	Y = 25	Z = 26		

1. Animal with a sum between 20 and 30 *Dog*

2. Food with a sum between 50 and 75 *Sushi*

3. Shape with a sum greater than 75 *rectangle*

34

Name _____ Date _____

Number Place

Round each number to its greatest place.

1,488 ___1,500___   435,456 ___435,460___

12,861 ___13,000___   922 ___920___

86,001 ___86,000___   277,005 ___277,005___

FAST Math

Round each number to its greatest place.
Then estimate each difference.

$$
\begin{array}{r}
71,826 \\
-\ 23,241 \\
\hline
\end{array}
\qquad
\begin{array}{r}
6,038 \\
-\ 497 \\
\hline
\end{array}
\qquad
\begin{array}{r}
668,721 \\
-\ 209,508 \\
\hline
\end{array}
$$

50,590

$$
\begin{array}{r}
29,244 \\
-\ 4,892 \\
\hline
24,752
\end{array}
\qquad
\begin{array}{r}
578,334 \\
-\ 416,009 \\
\hline
164,325
\end{array}
\qquad
\begin{array}{r}
800,896 \\
-\ 27,528 \\
\hline
773,160
\end{array}
$$

Think Tank

Anna's room is a rectangle. Its length is 15 feet and its width is 4 yards. What is the perimeter of the room?

___54___

Show your work in the tank.

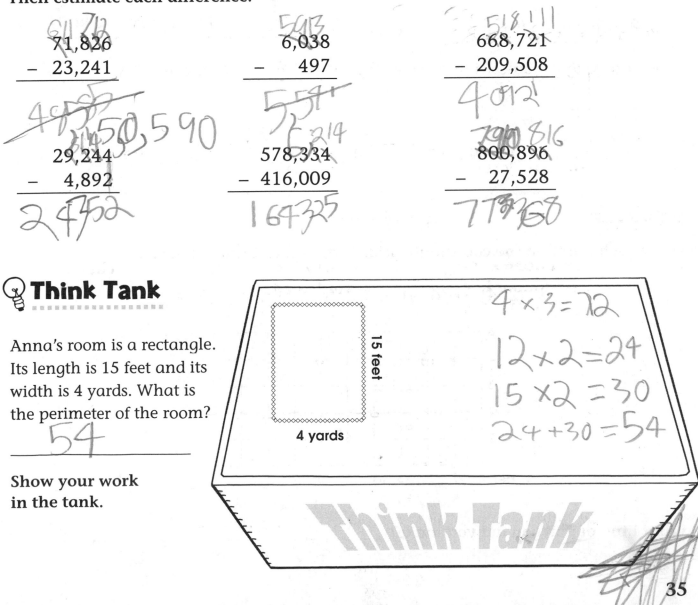

15 feet

4 yards

$4 \times 3 = 12$

$12 \times 2 = 24$

$15 \times 2 = 30$

$24 + 30 = 54$

Data Place

LaTanya's family runs a small jewelry kiosk at the mall. The list shows the prices of some of the items they sell.

Use the price list to answer the questions.

Item	Price
Ring	$49.95
Bracelet	$34.99
Watch	$75.00
Earrings	$20.49
Necklace	$185.99

1. How much does it cost to buy 10 watches?

720.00

2. How much more than a ring does a necklace cost? *136.40*

3. Which items differ in price by about $40? *watch and bracelet*

4. Lisa bought a bracelet and two watches. How much did she spend?

184.99

5. Clark spent $70.44. Which 2 items did he buy? *Ring and necklace*

Puzzler

Draw each point on the coordinate grid. Then connect them in order.

$$(2, 4) \rightarrow (6, 4) \rightarrow (8, 2) \rightarrow (4, 2) \rightarrow (2, 4)$$

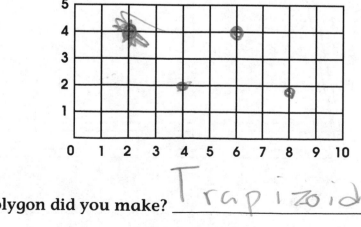

What kind of polygon did you make? *Trapizoid*

JUMPSTART 15

Side A

Name ______________________ Date ______________

Number Place

Round to the place of the underlined digit.

$\underline{9}31{,}488$ ______________

$192{,}8\underline{6}6$ ______________

$8\underline{0}6{,}001$ ______________

$\underline{4}35{,}465$ ______________

$922{,}\underline{0}07$ ______________

$2\underline{3}7{,}400$ ______________

FAST Math

Add or subtract.

$8.26 + $3.41	$.38 − $.29	$87.06 + $35.48
$912.44 − $48.92	$783.04 − $160.09	$218.26 + $35.41

Think Tank

Kim's backyard is 9 meters wide. It is twice as long as it is wide. What is the perimeter of the yard?

____

Show your work in the tank.

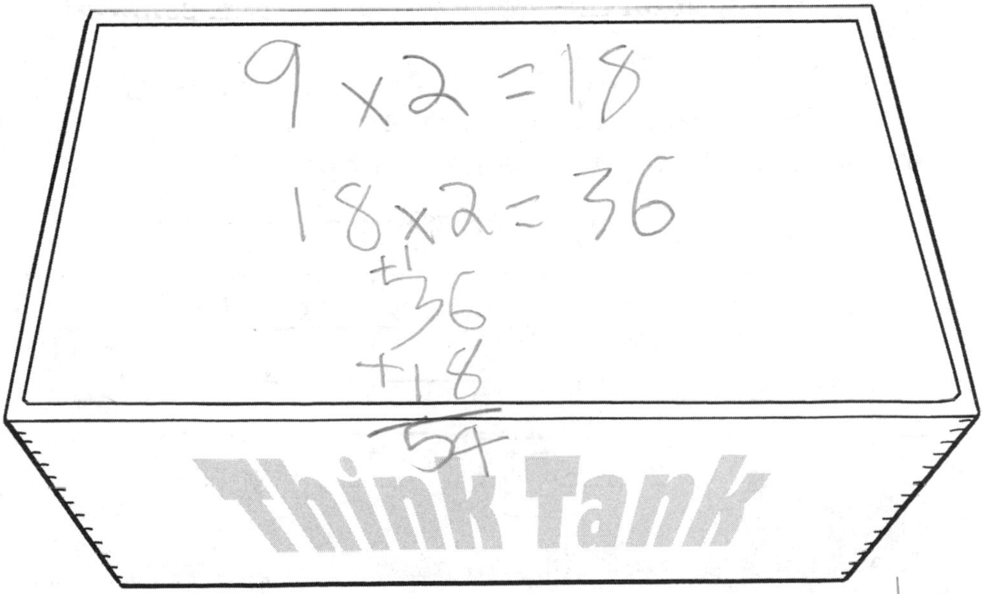

Data Place

What did your classmates have for breakfast today?

Pick 4 breakfast items to count and tally. Then graph the results.

Breakfast Item	Tally
Scrambledeggs	7
toast	3
waffles	10
Pancakes	4

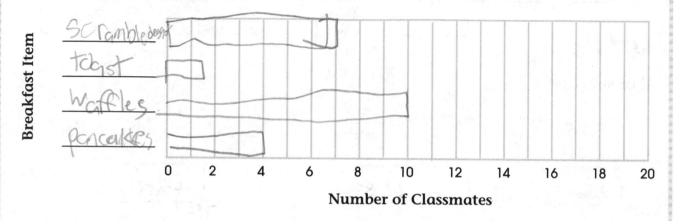

Breakfast Item: Scramble eggs, toast, Waffles, Pancakes

Number of Classmates: 0 2 4 6 8 10 12 14 16 18 20

What was hardest about this activity? ___Nothing___

Puzzler

Each problem has some missing digits.

**Use number sense to fill them in correctly.
Each of the digits 0–9 is missing only *once*.**

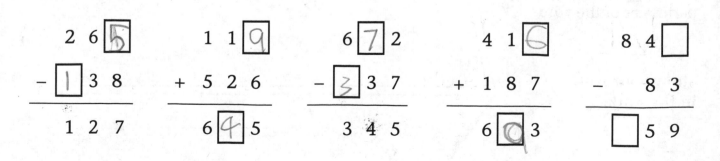

```
   2 6 [5]       1 1 [9]       6 [7] 2       4 1 [6]       8 4 [ ]
 - [1] 3 8     + 5 2 6       - [3] 3 7     + 1 8 7       -   8 3
 ---------     ---------     ---------     ---------     ---------
   1 2 7         6 [4] 5       3 4 5         6 [0] 3       [ ] 5 9
```

Morning Jumpstarts: Math, Grade 4 © 2013 by Scholastic Teaching Resources

Name _____ Date _____

Number Place

Write each number in expanded form.

2,382 _____ 2000 + 300 + 80 + 2

40,306 _____ 40,000 + 0,000 + 300 + 6

225,960 _____ 200,000 + 20,000 + 5,000 900 + 60 + 0

600,010 _____ 600,000 + 00,000 + 0,000 + 000 + 10 + 0

FAST Math

Estimate each sum or difference.

$82.26
+ $29.45

$42.18
− $6.89

$787.06
+ $395.44

$622.42
− $278.92

$783.04
− $160.09

$218.26
$488.16
+ $35.41

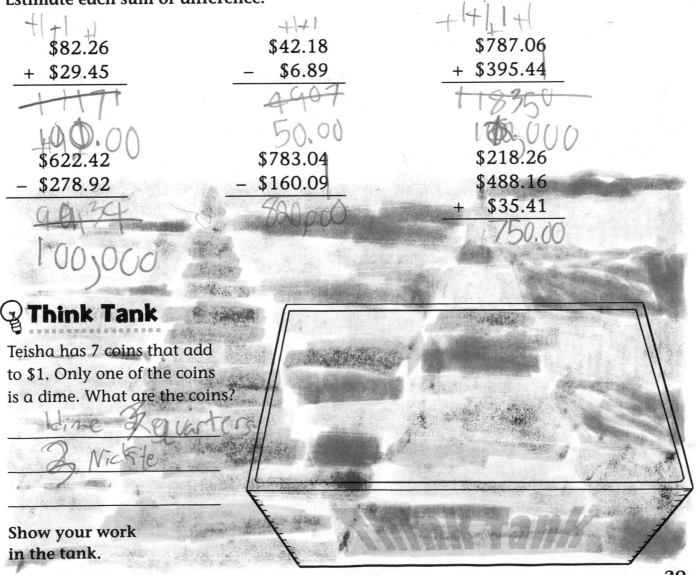

Think Tank

Teisha has 7 coins that add to $1. Only one of the coins is a dime. What are the coins?

Dime 3 Quarters
3 Nickle

Show your work in the tank.

Data Place

Make a Venn diagram with numbers between 0 and 50. Write multiples of 3 in one region. Write multiples of 5 in the other region. Write multiples of both 3 and 5 in the overlapping region.

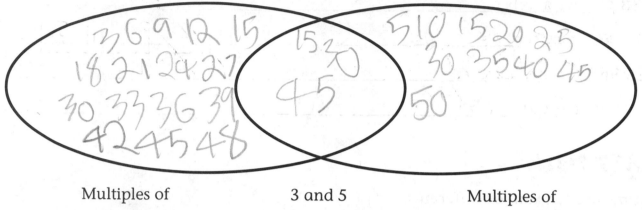

3 6 9 12 15
18 21 24 27
30 33 36 39
42 45 48

15 30
45

5 10 15 20 25
30 35 40 45
50

| Multiples of 3 only | 3 and 5 | Multiples of 5 only |

Puzzler

Fill in this design using 4 different colors. You can repeat colors—but not where sections touch.

40

Morning Jumpstarts: Math, Grade 4 © 2013 by Scholastic Teaching Resources

Name _____ Date _____

Number Place

Use all the numbers on the cards to form:

6	1	5
2	7	3

- the *greatest* number   765,321
- the *least* number   123,567
- the greatest *even* number   765,132
- the greatest *odd* number   765,321

FAST Math

Find each product as quickly as you can.

$3 \times 9 =$ 27 $5 \times 6 =$ 30 $7 \times 4 =$ 28

$5 \times 8 =$ 40 $4 \times 0 =$ 0 $4 \times 9 =$ 36

$6 \times 7 =$ 42 $1 \times 3 =$ 3 $7 \times 6 =$ 42

💡 Think Tank

What is the perimeter of Tran's apartment?

_____ 71 ft _____

Show your work in the tank.

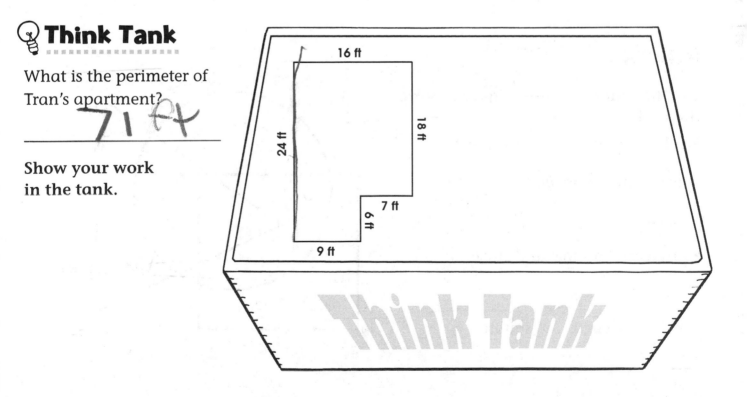

16 ft   18 ft   24 ft   7 ft   6 ft   9 ft

Think Tank

Data Place

Use the map of Veggie County to answer the questions.

All distances on the map are given in kilometers.

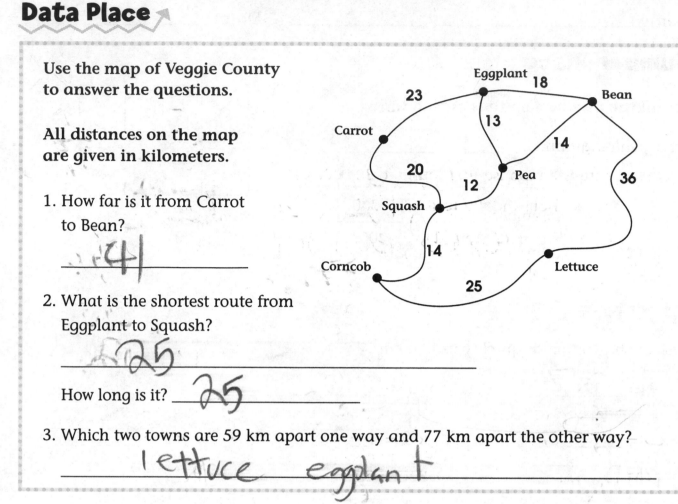

1. How far is it from Carrot to Bean?

   _____ 41 _____

2. What is the shortest route from Eggplant to Squash?

   _____ 25 _____

   How long is it? _____ 25 _____

3. Which two towns are 59 km apart one way and 77 km apart the other way?

   _____ lettuce   eggplant _____

Puzzler

Use the numbers in the figure to solve the problems below.

Find the product of numbers:

• inside the square *only*

   149

• inside the triangle and circle

   180

• inside the circle and square

   324

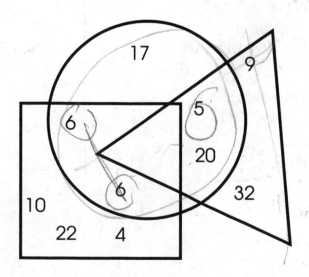

Morning Jumpstarts: Math, Grade 4 © 2013 by Scholastic Teaching Resources

Name _____ Date _____

Number Place

Read the clues to figure out the number.

- I am a 5-digit number.
- To the nearest ten-thousand, I round to 30,000.
- To the nearest thousand, I round to 27,000.
- To the nearest hundred, I round to 27,200.
- Four of my digits are 2s.

What number am I? ___27222___

FAST Math

Find each product as quickly as you can.

8 × 9 = __72__   5 × 9 = __45__   7 × 7 = __49__

7 × 8 = __56__   6 × 0 = __0__   9 × 7 = __63__

8 × 1 = __8__   9 × 9 = __81__   8 × 6 = __48__

Think Tank

Together, Iris and Ivan weigh 120 pounds. Iris weighs 10 pounds less than Ivan. How much does each child weigh?

Iris 50

Ivan 70

Show your work in the tank.

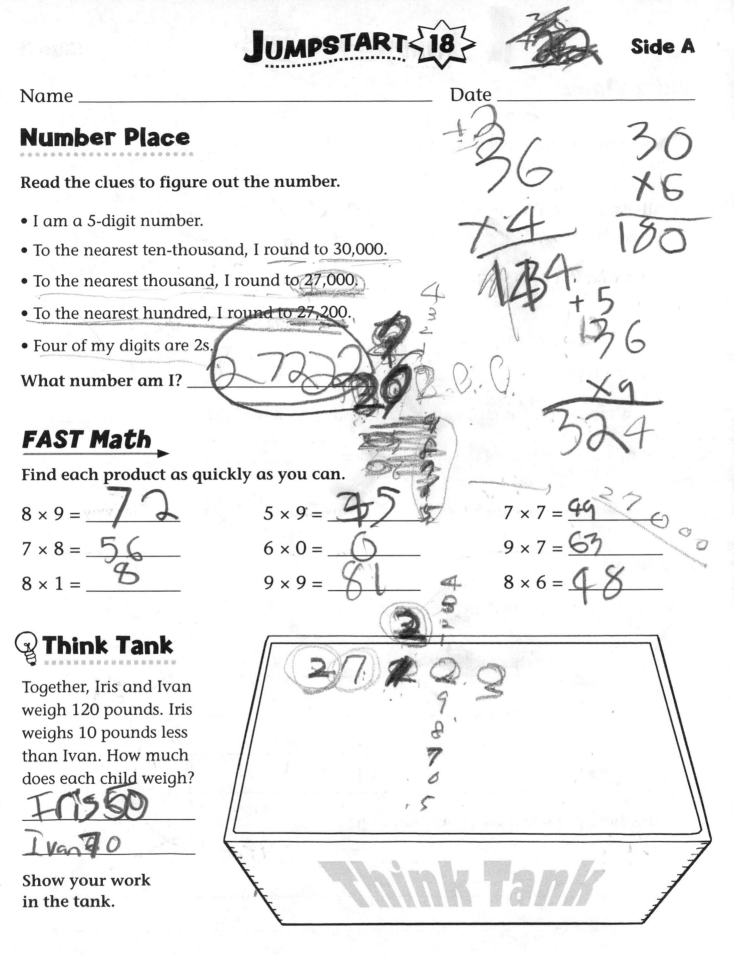

Data Place

Use the graph to answer the
questions about different
pets students have.

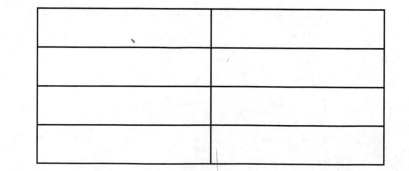

Students' Pets

Dogs 24 | Cats 12 | Fish 6 | Birds 6

1. How many students have
   either a bird or a dog? **30**

2. What kind of pet do
   $\frac{1}{4}$ of the students have? **Cats**

3. How many times as many students have dogs as have fish? **4**

4. Why is the dog part of the graph the largest? **the students have the most dogs**

Puzzler

How many rectangles are there in this figure?

Describe how you organized your thinking.

8 small 4 medium 1 huge

Name _____ Date _____

Number Place

Round each money amount to the nearest dollar *and* ten dollars.

Amount	Nearest $1	Nearest $10
$6.17	6 $	10 $
$28.62	29 $	30 $
$843.45	843 $	840 $

FAST Math

Break apart the factor in the rectangle to find the product.

$\boxed{7} \times 8 =$ (~~5~~ × 8) + (2 × 8)

7×8 =   40 + 16

56 =   56

$\boxed{6} \times 7 =$ (5 × 7) + (1 × 7)

6×7 =   35 + 7

42 =   42

$\boxed{6} \times 9 =$ (5 × 9) + (1 × 9)

6×9 =   45 + 9

54 =   54

$\boxed{7} \times 9 =$ (3 × 9) + (4 × 9)

7×9 =   27 + 27

63 =   63

Think Tank

Ari left the airport at 11:45 A.M. He drove for 55 minutes to get home. What time did he arrive?

12:40

Show your work in the tank.

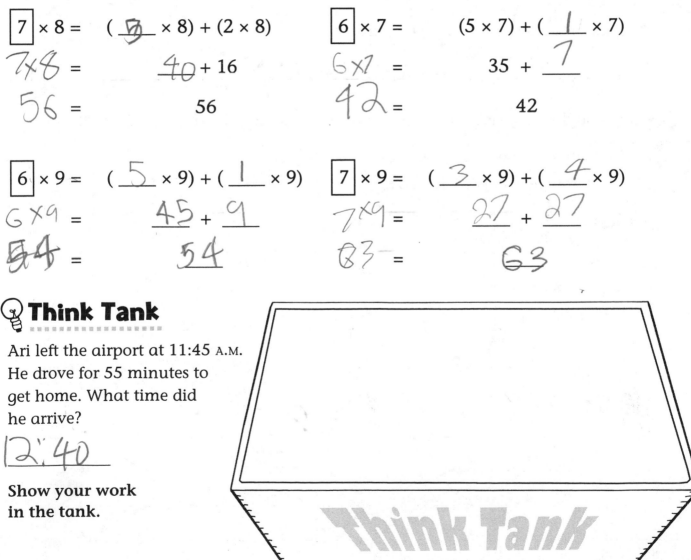

Data Place

Use the table about stadium seats to answer the questions.

Seats in a Stadium

Location	Number	Price
Field Level	8,000	$55
Mezzanine	5,600	$45
Loge	18,000	$35
Upper Deck	30,000	$25
Bleachers	800	$10

1. How many seats are in the stadium?

   63,400

2. How many more seats are in the upper deck than in the loge?

   12,000

3. What is the cost of 4 tickets in the mezzanine?

   160$

4. Cal bought 3 tickets for $105. Where are his seats? 2 upper deck Field level

5. Mia bought 2 tickets in one section and 2 in another. She spent $160 in all. Where are her seats? 2 upper 2 Field level

Puzzler

Begin at the ★.

Skip count by 9s to connect the dots.

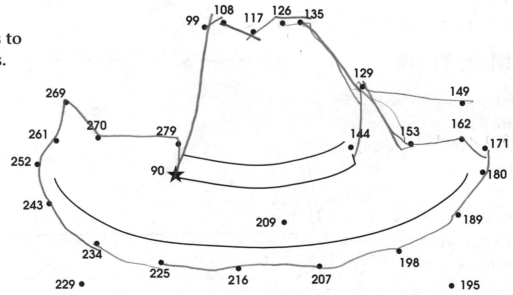

July 17

Name _____ Date _____

Number Place

Round each money amount to the nearest $100 _and_ $1,000.

Amount	Nearest $100	Nearest $1,000
$695.32	$700.00	$1,000
$1,230.55	$1,000.00	1,000.00
$6,843.45	$690.00	7,000.00

FAST Math

Multiply.

$3 \times 40 = 120$ $4 \times 50 = 200$ $3 \times 80 = 2400$ $6 \times 30 = 180$

$5 \times 70 = 350$ $3 \times 400 = 1200$ $5 \times 600 = 3000$ $4 \times 500 = 200$

$7 \times 300 = 2100$ $8 \times 600 = 4800$ $2 \times 900 = 1800$ $6 \times 700 = 4400$

Think Tank

What is the product of all numbers on a telephone key pad?

45

Explain how you know.

1 + 2 = 3   3 + 3 = 6
6 + 4 = 10   10 + 5 = 15
15 + 6 = 21   21 + 7 = 28
28 + 8 = 36   36 + 9 = 45

Data Place

Use the graph about dog food in stock at Pam's Pets during a 5-week period to answer the questions.

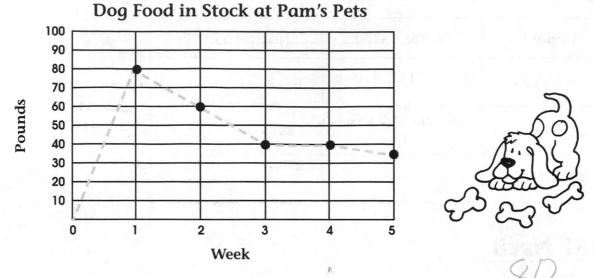

Dog Food in Stock at Pam's Pets

1. How many pounds of dog food did the store have in the first week? __80__

   In the third week? __40__

2. How much less dog food was in stock in the fourth week than in the second week?

   __20__

3. Describe the change in the amount of dog food from weeks 1 to 5.

   ___80 to 45___

Puzzler

You will water Ms. Gold's plants each day for 10 days. She says, "I can pay you $10 a day. Or, I can pay you 25¢ the first day, and then double the amount each day after that."

Which plan should you take? Finish the table to help you decide.

Day	1	2	3	4	5	6	7	8	9	10
Pay	$.25	$.50	$1	2	4	8	16	32	64	128

1. How much would you earn at $10 a day? __100__

2. How much would you earn with the doubling plan? __128__

48

Morning Jumpstarts: Math, Grade 4 © 2013 by Scholastic Teaching Resources

Name _____ Date _____

Number Place

Rewrite each money amount. Use $ and .

four dollars and sixty cents ___4.60$___

twenty-seven dollars and thirty-four cents ___$27.34___

one hundred ninety dollars and two cents ___$190.00___

two thousand fifteen dollars and fifty cents ___$2005.50___

FAST Math

Multiply.

$8 \times 6,000 =$ ___48000___ $6 \times 4,000 =$ ___24000___ $3 \times 8,000 =$ ___24000___

$4 \times 7,000 =$ ___28000___ $5 \times 3,000 =$ ___15000___ $8 \times 9,000 =$ ___82000___

$9 \times 2,000 =$ ___18000___ $7 \times 8,000 =$ ___56000___ $8 \times 6,000 =$ ___48000___

Think Tank

Rosa saw ducks and cows at a farm. In all, she counted 9 animals and 28 legs. How many ducks and how many cows did she see?

___4 ducks___

___5 cows___

Show your work in the tank.

Data Place

The line plot shows the number of hours students said they spent reading each week.

Use the data in the line plot to answer the questions.

Hours Spent Reading

```
                X
                X
X               X
X   X   X   X
X   X   X   X
X   X   X   X   X
X   X   X   X   X   X
X   X   X   X   X   X               X
—————————————————————————————————————————
1   2   3   4   5   6   7   8   9   10
```

1. How many students were surveyed? _____30_____

2. What is the range of the data? ___6___

3. What is the mode of the data? ___3___

4. How many students say they read for 5 hours each week? ___3___

5. An outlier is a value that "lies outside" (or away from) the rest of the data.

   Which number of hours is an outlier? ___10___

Puzzler

Complete the category chart. The letters above each column tell the first letter for each word. Three are done for you.

Category	R	O	P	E	S
Number Words	**R**oman numeral	one	Pi	even	six
Measure Words	ruler	ounce	pound	**E**quivalent	scale
Geometry Words	rectangle	octogon	**P**olygon	equal	sides

50

JUMPSTART 22

Name _____ Date _____

Number Place

Compare. Write **<**, **=**, or **>**.

200,999 __<__ 209,000   150,551 __>__ 150,155

90,988 __<__ 100,000   908,444 __>__ 901,888

60,778 __<__ sixty thousand seven hundred eighty-five

four hundred fifty thousand __=__ 405,000

FAST Math

Round to the nearest 10 or 100. Then estimate the product.

3 × 68 = __210__   6 × 41 = __240__   2 × 807 = __1,620__

4 × 771 = __324,000__   5 × 380 = __1,900__   8 × 915 = __7,360__

7 × 27 = __210__   9 × 637 = __5760__   4 × 662 = __2680__

💡 Think Tank

Macaws can live to be about 64 years old. Hamsters live for about 4 years. About how many times longer than hamsters do macaws live?

__16__

Show your work in the tank.

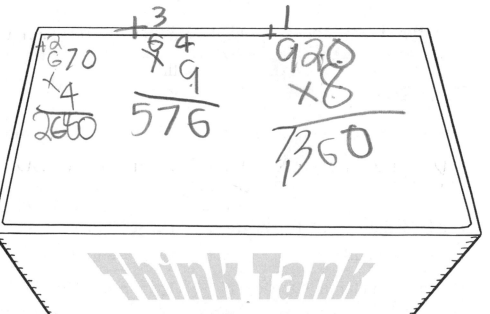

Data Place

The graph compares television sales at Ed's Electronics Store.

Use the graph to answer the questions.

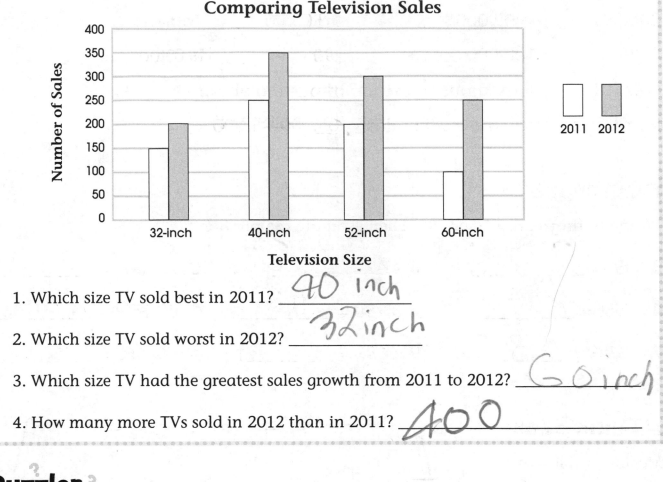

1. Which size TV sold best in 2011? _____40 inch_____

2. Which size TV sold worst in 2012? _____32 inch_____

3. Which size TV had the greatest sales growth from 2011 to 2012? _____60 inch_____

4. How many more TVs sold in 2012 than in 2011? _____400_____

Puzzler

Use the clues below to find out the home of the most famous groundhog in America.

P U N X S U T A W N E Y , PA

The second and sixth letters are *u*.

The fourth letter is *x*.

The third and tenth letters are *n*.

The eighth letter is *a*.

The twelfth letter is *y*.

The seventh letter is *t*.

The eleventh letter is *e*.

The ninth letter is *w*.

The first letter is *P*.

The fifth letter is *s*.

Morning Jumpstarts: Math, Grade 4 © 2013 by Scholastic Teaching Resources

Name _____ Date _____

Number Place

Compare. Write **<**, **=**, or **>**.

$20,000 __<__ $200,000 $150,500 __>__ $150,150

$998,008 __<__ $998,800 $90,999 __<__ $900,000

$667,000 __<__ six hundred seventy thousand dollars

four hundred five thousand dollars __>__ $405,000

FAST Math

Round to the greatest place. Then estimate the product.

5 × 658 = __3500__   7 × 431 = __3000__   2 × 8,107 = __16,200__

4 × 791 = __3200__   5 × 3,780 = __20,000__   3 × 9,150 = __27,450__

6 × 279 = __1800__   9 × 527 = __4770__   4 × 6,262 = __24,120__

Think Tank

There are 25 players on each Major League baseball team. There are 30 teams in all. How many players are in the Major Leagues?

__750__

Show your work in the tank.

Morning Jumpstarts: Math, Grade 4 © 2013 by Scholastic Teaching Resources

Data Place

Carlos rolled a 1–6 number cube 50 times.
He recorded his results in a tally table.

Complete the bar graph to display the results.

Results for 50 Rolls

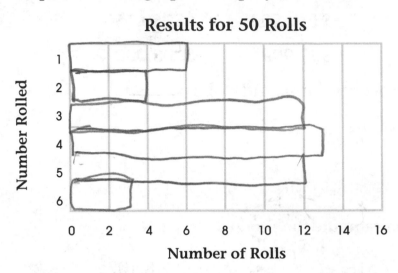

Number Rolled

Number of Rolls

What I Rolled	How Many
1	⟍⟍⟍⟍⟍ I
2	IIII
3	⟍⟍⟍⟍⟍ ⟍⟍⟍⟍⟍ II
4	⟍⟍⟍⟍⟍ ⟍⟍⟍⟍⟍ III
5	⟍⟍⟍⟍⟍ ⟍⟍⟍⟍⟍ II
6	III

1. Which two numbers came up the same number of times? _____

2. Which number came up the most often? _____

Puzzler

Each number has a different shape around it in the tic-tac-toe grid. For instance, ⊓ stands for 8. Do you see why?

Use this code to solve the problems.

1	2	3
4	5	6
7	8	9

1. ⊐ ⊐ × ⊐ = $\underline{264}$

2. ⊔ ⊔ × ⊔ = $\underline{104}$

3. ⊓ ⊔ ⊐ × ⊐ = $\underline{3296}$

4. ⊓ ⊔ ⊓ × ⊔ = $\underline{2484}$

Morning Jumpstarts: Math, Grade 4 © 2013 by Scholastic Teaching Resources

Name _____ Date _____

Number Place

Write any number that belongs between.

2,140 < __2,145__ < 2,150   51,400 > __51,399__ > 51,395

7,065 < __7,099__ < 7,100   60,001 > __59,999__ > 59,998

89,000 < __89,002__ < 89,003   30,078 > __30,077__ > 30,000

FAST Math →

Find each product. Circle the two products that are the same.

5 × 56 = __280__   4 × 91 = (__364__)   4 × 19 = __76__

6 × 702 = __4212__   6 × 316 = __1896__   8 × 68 = __484__

3 × 922 = __2766__   7 × 52 = (__364__)   7 × 751 = __5257__

💡 Think Tank

Forty-four runners from Thorpe School are going to a track meet. The vans that take them hold 8 students each. How many vans do the runners need?

____6____

Show your work in the tank.

+2
44
×6
264

8²4
× 4
____
3296

8²8
× 3
____
2484

Data Place

The Fish Tank is having a sale on some popular items.

Use the price list to answer the questions below.

1. How much more than the book does the tank cost? $25.35¢

2. Jae spent $29.73 on three items. What are they? _Fish Food, Tank Plantsunken ship_

3. Which costs more: 2 of the 20-gallon tanks or 6 sunken ships? _Sunken ships_

How much more? $6.6

Item	Price
Fish Food	$ 5.79
Tropical Fish Book	$15.25
Tank Plant	$10.99
20-Gallon Tank	$35.95
Sunken Ship	$12.95

Puzzler

In each shape, cross out the fraction or mixed number that does *not* belong.
Then, write one that *does* belong on the line beneath the shape.

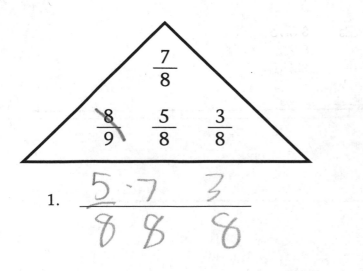

$$\frac{7}{8}$$

$$\frac{8}{9} \quad \frac{5}{8} \quad \frac{3}{8}$$

1. $\frac{5}{8} \quad \frac{7}{8} \quad \frac{3}{8}$

$$1\frac{4}{8} \qquad 1\frac{3}{6}$$

$$1\frac{2}{5} \qquad 1\frac{5}{10}$$

2. $1\frac{4}{8}$

Morning Jumpstarts: Math, Grade 4 © 2013 by Scholastic Teaching Resources

Name _____ Date _____

Number Place

Write the next 2 numbers in each pattern.

33   303   3,003   _30,003_   _300,003_

7,001   8,001   9,001   _10,001_   _11,001_

204   2,005   20,006   _200,007_   _2,000,008_

1,000,009   100,008   10,007   _1,006_   _105_

FAST Math

Multiply. Circle the two products that have a sum of 925.

5 × 36 = _340_   4 × 98 = _392_   4 × 397 = _1,588_

6 × 752 = _4512_   6 × 816 = _4,896_   8 × 78 = _684_

3 × 622 = _1,866_   7 × 43 = _301_   5 × 671 = _3,355_

Think Tank

Leon ordered two items from the catalog. His change from a $20 bill was $6.10. Which two items did he order?

top hat

mask

Show your work in the tank.

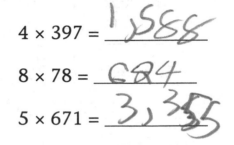

COSTUME SUPPLIES	
Top Hat	$ 4.79
Mask	$ 8.95
Bag of Eyeballs	$ 3.95
Whistle	$ 2.95
Fake Fangs	$ 4.19
Clown Shoes	$ 9.95

Jul 21

JUMPSTART 25

Side B

Data Place

Identify the coordinates for each ordered pair that forms the
square. Write them on the line below each grid.

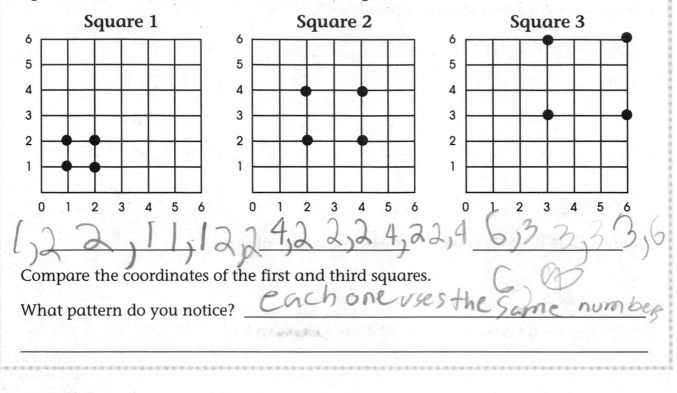

Square 1 **Square 2** **Square 3**

1,2 2,1 1,1 1,2   2,4 2,2 4,2 2,4 2,2 4,4   6,3 3,3 3,6 3,6

Compare the coordinates of the first and third squares.

What pattern do you notice? _each one uses the same number_

_____

Puzzler

The triangles have 9 boxes. Use the numbers 1–9 once
in each triangle. Write a number in each box so that
the sum on each side of the triangle is the same.

1. Make the *least* possible sum.   2. Make the *greatest* possible sum.

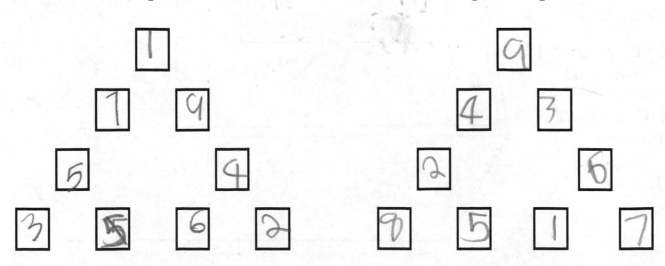

Left triangle:
1
7 9
5 4
3 5 6 2

Right triangle:
9
4 3
2 6
8 5 1 7

Side A

Name _____ Date _____

Number Place

Write the correct number from the box.

- It is the greatest number. _101,005_

- They are less than 8,000.
  _3,811   4,981_

- They are greater than 80,000
  _100,500   101,005   85_

- Circle the leftover numbers.

3,811	9,005
	10,500
8,005	20,530
	101,005
100,500	85,875
	4,981

FAST Math

Find each product. Circle any product that rounds to $3.

8 × $.45 = _3.60_

6 × $2.23 = _8.23_

9 × $3.39 = _30.51_

7 × $.40 = _2.80_

4 × $5.20 = _20.80_

3 × $.67 = _2.04_

1 × $7.00 = _7.00_

2 × $8.55 = _17.10_

5 × $9.82 = _49.10_

Think Tank

Brian's team scored 26 two-point baskets and 7 three-point baskets. How many points did his team score?

_76_

Show your work in the tank.

+4
45
× 8
360

Think Tank

Data Place

Forty-eight students took a homework survey. The table shows the results. But some of the table is blank.

Use the clues to complete the table.

• Four times as many students prefer working on the floor to working on the bed.

• Seven times as many students prefer working at a table to working on the bed.

Best Homework Spot	Tally	Number
bed	IIII	4
Floor	HH HH HH I	16
table	HH HH HH HH HH III	28

Puzzler

Tetrominoes are figures made of 4 squares joined flush along 1 or more sides. Two have been done as examples.

Draw four other tetrominoes on the grid.

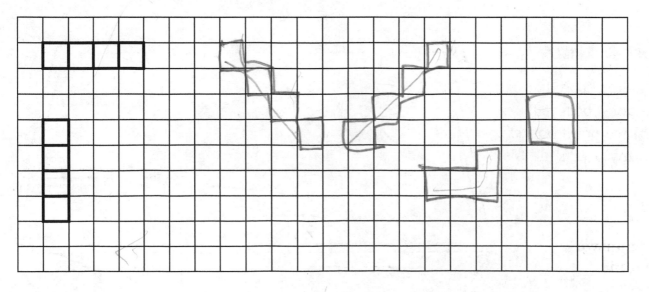

Morning Jumpstarts: Math, Grade 4 © 2013 by Scholastic Teaching Resources

Name _____ Date _____

Number Place

Write the decimal for each part.

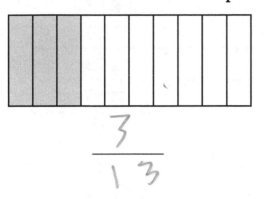

$$\frac{3}{13}$$

$$\frac{6}{10}$$

FAST Math ➤

Find each quotient as quickly as you can.

27 ÷ 3 = ___   18 ÷ 2 = ___   32 ÷ 4 = ___

30 ÷ 3 = ___   24 ÷ 4 = ___   0 ÷ 5 = ___

40 ÷ 5 = ___   30 ÷ 3 = ___   36 ÷ 4 = ___

💡 Think Tank

Rosa's teacher ordered 6 pizzas for a party. Each cost $12.75. She shared the cost equally with 4 other teachers. How much did each teacher pay?

_____

Show your work in the tank.

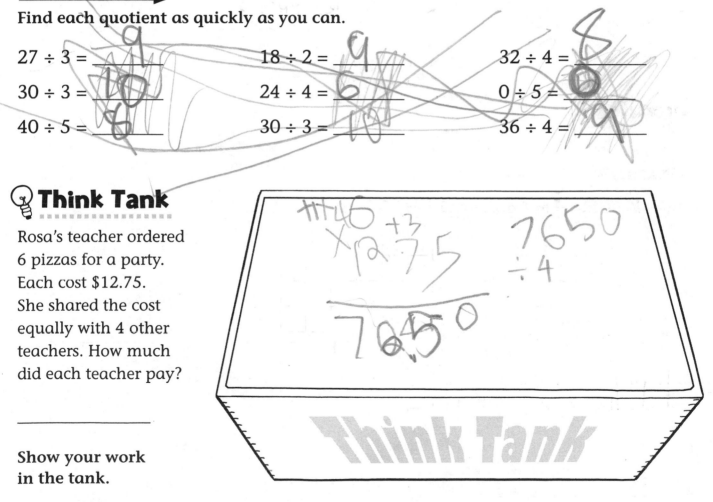

Think Tank

Data Place

Sue's Sign Shop is having a sale. The table shows the cost of placing words on a sign. You pay by the letter. Prices vary by letter heights.

Use the table to answer the questions.

Letter Height	Price per Letter
1 inch	$.75
3 inches	$1.50
6 inches	$2.75
9 inches	$4.00
12 inches	$5.50

1. What would it cost for a sign with your first and last names in 3-inch letters? _$16.50_

2. What would it cost for a sign with the name of your school in 12-inch letters? _$60.50_

3. Alex got a sign that says VOTE FOR ME. He spent $24.75. What size letters did he get? _6 inches_

Puzzler

Choose one number from each box to find each product.

Box A

316		649
88	447	205

×

Box B

5		4
3	6	2

1. _447_ × _5_ = 2,235
     A   B

2. _649_ × _2_ = 1,264
     A   B

Morning Jumpstarts: Math, Grade 4 © 2013 by Scholastic Teaching Resources

Name _____ Date _____

Number Place

Write the decimal for each part.

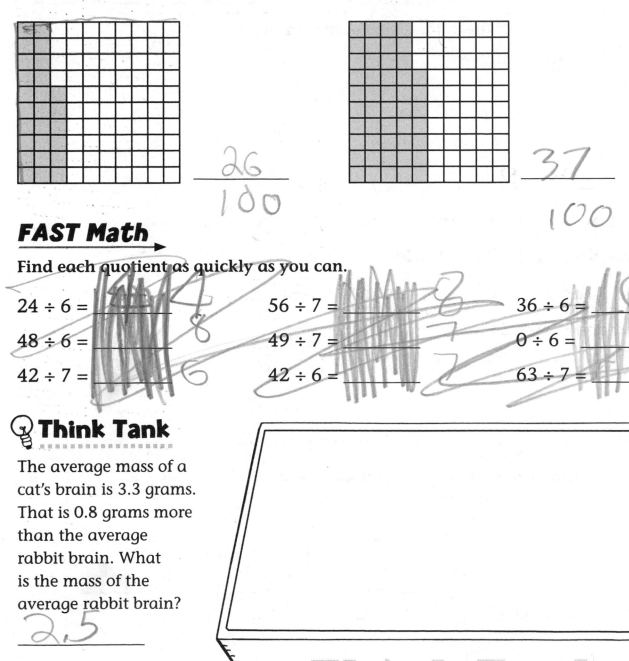

$\dfrac{26}{100}$

$\dfrac{37}{100}$

FAST Math

Find each quotient as quickly as you can.

$24 \div 6 =$ _____ $56 \div 7 =$ _____ $36 \div 6 =$ _____

$48 \div 6 =$ _____ $49 \div 7 =$ _____ $0 \div 6 =$ _____

$42 \div 7 =$ _____ $42 \div 6 =$ _____ $63 \div 7 =$ _____

💡 Think Tank

The average mass of a cat's brain is 3.3 grams. That is 0.8 grams more than the average rabbit brain. What is the mass of the average rabbit brain?

2.5

_____

Show your work in the tank.

Think Tank

Morning Jumpstarts: Math, Grade 4 © 2013 by Scholastic Teaching Resources

Data Place

Nita runs a kennel. The table shows the kinds of dogs at the kennel today.

Dog Breed	Boxer	Collie	Hound	Mutt	Terrier
Number	28	32	30	48	22

Make a pictograph of the data. Give it a title and a key.

Use  **to stand for 4 dogs.**

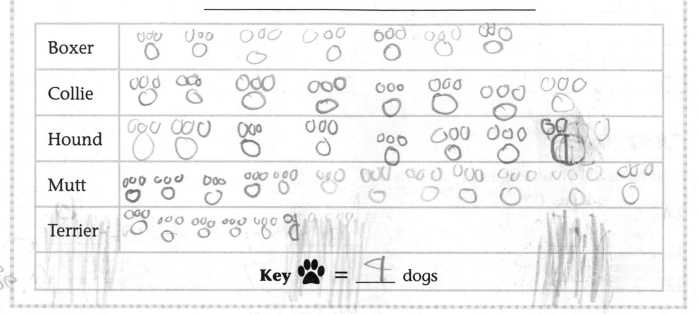

Boxer	
Collie	
Hound	
Mutt	
Terrier	

Key 🐾 = ___4___ dogs

Puzzler

Use the fraction code to spell two different math words.
Write the letters in the order they appear in the clue.

The last $\frac{2}{5}$ of **triad**

The last $\frac{1}{3}$ of **parade**

The middle $\frac{1}{3}$ of **wander**

addend

The last $\frac{1}{5}$ of **catch**

The last $\frac{1}{2}$ of **apex**

The first $\frac{1}{3}$ of **agreed**

The second $\frac{2}{3}$ of **son**

hexagon

Make up your own fraction code to spell your last name. Use another sheet of paper.

 **Side A**

Name _____ Date _____

Number Place

Circle each number that has a 4 in the tenths place.

4.5   7.4   23.04   (40.43)

Circle each number that has a 4 in the hundredths place.

4.05   7.14   24.04   30.47

Circle each number that does not have a 4 in the tenths or hundredths place.

(4.01)   7.14   (84.04)   40.32

FAST Math

Find each quotient as quickly as you can.

$32 \div 8 =$ _____ $36 \div 9 =$ _____ $40 \div 10 =$ _____
$63 \div 9 =$ _____ $45 \div 9 =$ _____ $64 \div 8 =$ _____
$60 \div 10 =$ _____ $48 \div 8 =$ _____ $56 \div 8 =$ _____

Think Tank

Jada bought a 64-ounce container of apple juice. How many full 6-ounce glasses of juice can she serve her friends?

__10__

Show your work in the tank.

Think Tank

Morning Jumpstarts: Math, Grade 4 © 2013 by Scholastic Teaching Resources

Data Place

Students named the continent they most want to visit.

Use the graph to answer the questions.

Continents to Visit

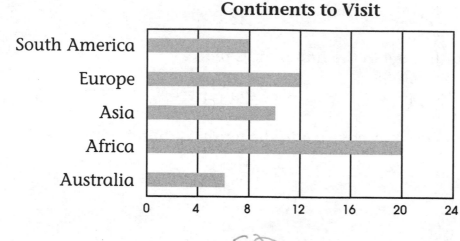

1. How many students voted? ___50___

2. Which continent got more than twice the number of votes South America did?

___Africa___

3. How many more students chose Africa than Europe? ___8___

Puzzler

Draw a picture to help you solve this money puzzle.

Matsu put 12 pennies in a row on his desk.

Then he swapped every 2nd penny for a quarter.

Next, he swapped every 3rd coin for a dime.

Finally, he swapped every 4th coin for a nickel.

1. How much money is on the desk now?

___$1.41___

2. How much more is it than Matsu started with?

___1.29___

Morning Jumpstarts: Math, Grade 4 © 2013 by Scholastic Teaching Resources

Name _____ Date _____

Number Place

Write each decimal in number form.

three tenths _____$\frac{3}{10}$_____

sixty-two hundredths _____$\frac{62}{100}$_____

nine tenths _____$\frac{9}{10}$_____

seven hundredths _____$\frac{7}{100}$_____

sixteen hundredths _____$\frac{16}{100}$_____

one hundredth _____$\frac{1}{100}$_____

FAST Math ➤

Find the missing numbers.

If $3 \times 9 = 27$, then $3 \times 90 =$ ___270___ .

If $6 \times 8 =$ ___48___ , then $6 \times 80 =$ ___480___ .

If $7 \times 7 =$ ___49___ , then $7 \times 70 =$ ___490___ and $7 \times 700 =$ ___4,900___ .

If $35 \div 5 = 7$, then $350 \div 5 =$ ___70___ .

If $54 \div 9 =$ ___5___ , then $540 \div 9 =$ ___50___ .

If $32 \div 4 =$ ___8___ , then $320 \div 4 =$ ___80___ and $3,200 \div 4 =$ ___800___ .

💡 Think Tank

An oak tree is 5.5 meters tall. An elm tree is 1.1 meters shorter. How tall is the elm tree?

_____4.4_____

Show your work in the tank.

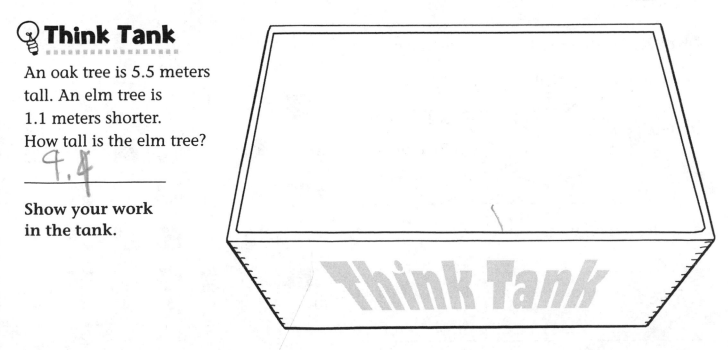

Data Place

Use the graph about building heights to answer the questions.

Building Heights (in stories)

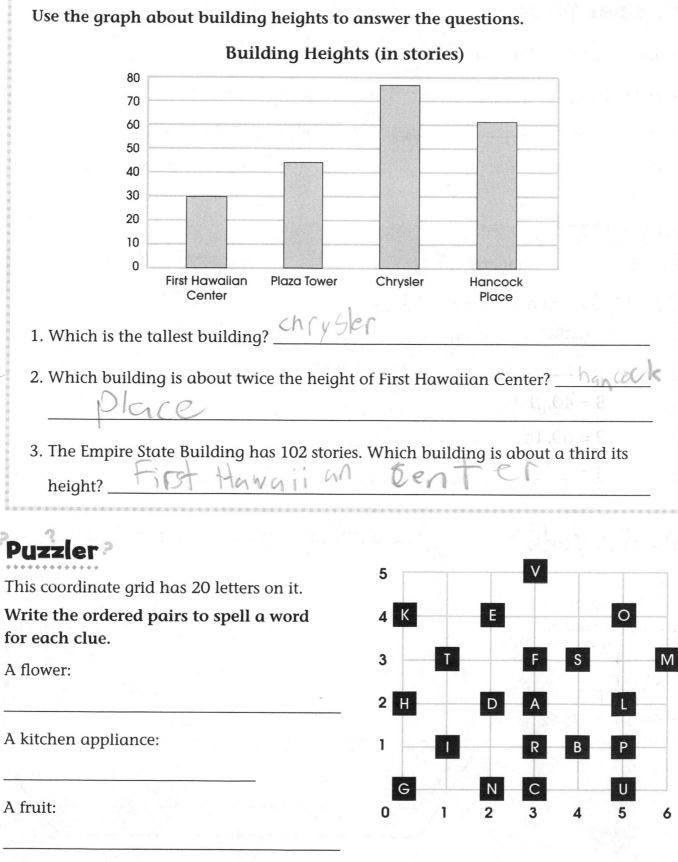

1. Which is the tallest building? _chrysler_

2. Which building is about twice the height of First Hawaiian Center? _hancock Place_

3. The Empire State Building has 102 stories. Which building is about a third its height? _First Hawaiian center_

Puzzler

This coordinate grid has 20 letters on it.

Write the ordered pairs to spell a word for each clue.

A flower:

_____

A kitchen appliance:

_____

A fruit:

_____

68

Name _____ Date _____

Number Place

Compare. Write **<**, **=**, or **>**.

2.5 __7__ 0.5   1.5 __<__ 1.8

3.7 __<__ 7.3   39.4 __<__ 39

60.7 __<__ sixty-seven   9.6 __=__ nine and six tenths

FAST Math ▶

Find the missing numbers in the fact family patterns.

If 3 × 50 = 150, then 150 ÷ 3 = __50__ .

If 6 × 70 = 420, then 420 ÷ 6 = __70__ .

If 7 × 40 = __240__ , then __240__ ÷ 7 = 40.

If 320 ÷ 8 = 40, then 8 × 40 = __320__ .

If 540 ÷ 9 = 60, then 9 × 60 = __540__ .

If 400 ÷ 4 = __100__ , then 4 × 100 = __400__ .

💡 Think Tank

The first modern Olympics was held in 1896. The winning time in the 100-meter dash was 12 seconds. In 2008 the winning time was 9.69 seconds. How much faster was the 2008 winning time?

_____

Show your work in the tank.

Data Place

The line plot shows students' science test scores. Use the data to answer the questions.

Science Test Scores

```
                                              X
                                              X
                                              X
                                         X    X
                                         X    X    X
                                    X    X    X    X    X
                 X                  X    X    X    X    X    X
  ─────────────────────────────────────────────────────────────────
  0    5   10   15   20   25   30   35   40   45   50   55   60   65   70   75   80   85   90   95  100
```

1. How many students took the test? _____ *20*

2. What is the range of the data? _____ *50*

3. What is the mode of the data? _____ *6*

4. How many students scored lower than 80? _____ *7*

5. Which score is an outlier? _____ *45* _____ How do you know?
   If is way away from the others

Puzzler

Write the numbers 1,000, 2,000, 3,000, 4,000, and 5,000 *once* each in the five boxes. Make the sum of the three numbers in each direction total 10,000.

How did you solve the problem?
2+5+3=10   1+4+5=10
_____

2,000
1,000 5,000 4,000
3,000

70

Morning Jumpstarts: Math, Grade 4 © 2013 by Scholastic Teaching Resources

August 5 **Side A**

Name _____ Date _____

Number Place

Order the decimals from *least* to *greatest*.

1.6   1.2   1.9   1.5

6.4   6.7   6.8   6.1

6.8 6.7 6.4 6.1 ~~1.9~~ 1.9
1.6 1.5 1.2

Order the decimals from *greatest* to *least*.

10.1   10.9   0.4   10.6

12.7   12.3   11.9   12.8

12.8 12.7 12.3 11.9
10.9 10.6 10.1 0.4

FAST Math

Use number sense to estimate each quotient.

37 ÷ 8 = __5__   34 ÷ 9 = __3__   429 ÷ 7 = _____

624 ÷ 9 = _____   155 ÷ 4 = _____   650 ÷ 8 = _____

29 ÷ 4 = __7R2__   428 ÷ 6 = _____   493 ÷ 5 = _____

Think Tank

How many seconds are there in 2 hours?

 ~~2,400~~

Show your work in the tank.

60
×60
‾‾‾‾
1200

71

Data Place

Students counted the number of cousins they have.

Finish the table. Then answer the questions below.

Number of Cousins

Range	Tallies	Number
0–4	卌 II	7
5–8	卌 卌 卌 卌 卌 卌 卌 卌 II	42
9–12	卌 卌 卌 卌 I	21
13–16	卌 卌 卌 II	17
17 or more	卌 IIII	9

1. Which range has three times as many tallies as 0–4? __9—12__

2. Which range has half as many tallies as 5–8? __9—12__

3. Which range would include the number of cousins you have?

__0—4__

Puzzler

**Half a design appears on one side of a line of symmetry.
Complete the rest of the design. Keep it symmetric.**

Morning Jumpstarts: Math, Grade 4 © 2013 by Scholastic Teaching Resources

Name _____ Date _____

Number Place

Compare. Write **<**, **=**, or **>**.

2.05 ___>___ 0.05   1.35 ___<___ 1.38

3.71 ___>___ 3.70   49.60 ___>___ 49.06

6.47 ___<___ sixty-four and seventy hundredths

three and eighteen hundredths ___=___ 3.18

FAST Math

Use number sense to estimate each quotient.

389 ÷ 8 = _____   314 ÷ 6 = _____   4,166 ÷ 7 = _____

173 ÷ 3 = _____   3,572 ÷ 4 = _____   3,177 ÷ 8 = _____

6,341 ÷ 9 = _____   2,439 ÷ 6 = _____   3,583 ÷ 5 = _____

Think Tank

A golfer hit a 250-yard shot and then a 130-yard shot to the hole. How many feet did she hit the ball, in total?

___380___

Show your work in the tank.

Think Tank

Data Place

The table provides data on school populations.

Display the data in a bar graph. Give your graph a title and add the labels.

School	Populations
Chavez	976
McAuliffe	723
Rita Dove	1,020
Whitman	897

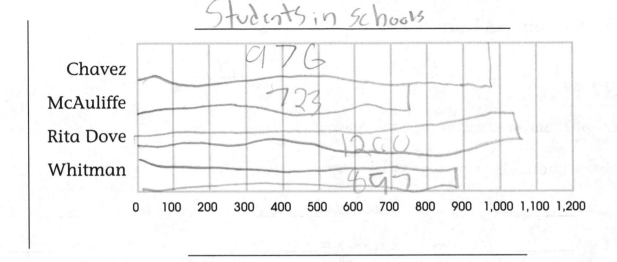

Students in schools

Chavez — 976
McAuliffe — 723
Rita Dove — 1200
Whitman — 897

Write the school names in population order from largest to smallest.

Rita Dove, Chavez, Whitman, McAuliffe

Puzzler

Try this toothpick challenge.
Rearrange the 12 toothpicks to
make 3 squares that are
congruent (the same size and shape).

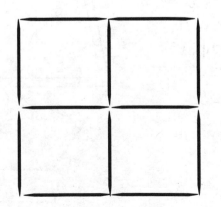

Morning Jumpstarts: Math, Grade 4 © 2013 by Scholastic Teaching Resources

Name _____ Date _____

Number Place

Order the decimals from *least* to *greatest*.

1.06   1.02   1.92   1.05   _1.02   1.05   1.06   1.92_

6.43   6.73   4.47   6.14   _4.47 6.14 6.43 6.73_

Order the decimals from *greatest* to *least*.

10.01   10.91   9.99   10.06   _12.37   12.23 11.23_

12.37   11.23   10.16   12.23   _10.91 10.16 10.6 10.1 9.99_

FAST Math ➤

Find each quotient.

72 ÷ 3 = _____   48 ÷ 2 = _____   64 ÷ 4 = _____

98 ÷ 7 = _____   114 ÷ 3 = _____   126 ÷ 6 = _____

255 ÷ 5 = _____   176 ÷ 8 = _____   288 ÷ 9 = _____

💡 Think Tank

A punch recipe calls for
3 quarts of cranberry juice,
1 quart of orange juice,
and 1 gallon of club soda.
How many cups of
cranberry juice does
the recipe need?

_____64 cups_____

**Show your work
in the tank.**

Data Place

The table shows the estimated populations of America's five largest cities, as of April 2010.

Use the table to answer the questions.

City	Population
New York, NY	8,175,133
Los Angeles, CA	3,792,621
Chicago, IL	2,695,598
Houston, TX	2,099,451
Philadelphia, PA	1,526,006

1. Which city's population rounds to 3,000,000?

   Chicago

2. Which two cities differ in population by about 1,700,000? _Houston, los-_
   angeles

3. Which city has about 3 times as many people as Chicago? _New York_

4. Suppose Philadelphia's population increases by about 500,000. About how many
   people would live there? _2,000,000_

Puzzler

Color the design.
Use the key.

If the decimal is	Color the space
> 1.0	blue
= 0.5	purple
< 0.5	green

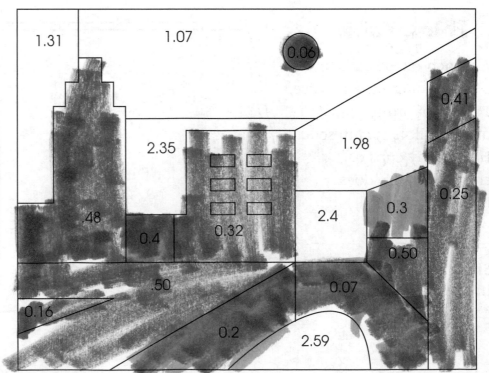

Name _____ Date _____

Number Place

Finish labeling the number line to show equivalent decimals and fractions.

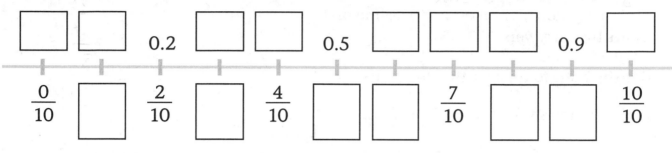

| | | 0.2 | | | 0.5 | | | | | 0.9 | |

$\frac{0}{10}$ | | $\frac{2}{10}$ | | $\frac{4}{10}$ | | | $\frac{7}{10}$ | | | $\frac{10}{10}$

FAST Math

Find each quotient.

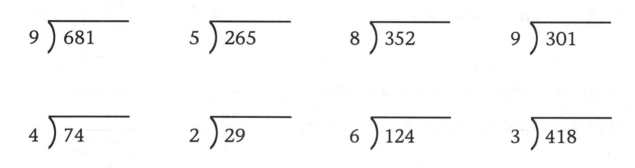

$9\overline{)681}$ $5\overline{)265}$ $8\overline{)352}$ $9\overline{)301}$

$4\overline{)74}$ $2\overline{)29}$ $6\overline{)124}$ $3\overline{)418}$

Think Tank

Luz played soccer for $2\frac{3}{4}$ hours on Monday and for $1\frac{1}{4}$ hours on Tuesday. How much longer did Luz play on Monday?

$1\frac{1}{2}$

Show your work in the tank.

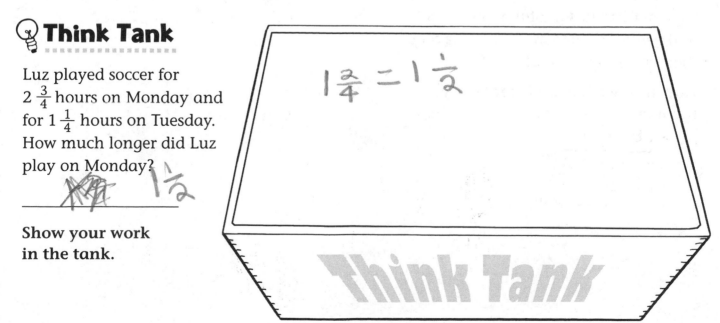

$1\frac{2}{4} = 1\frac{1}{2}$

Think Tank

Data Place

Mr. Bunsen's students are working on science projects. He asks them to describe how far along they are. "Are you closest to $\frac{1}{4}$ done, $\frac{1}{2}$ done, $\frac{3}{4}$ done, or all done?" The line plot shows their answers.

Science Project Status

```
                          X
                          X
                          X
                    X     X
                    X     X
                    X     X
                    X     X
                    X     X
              X     X     X
              X     X     X
              X     X     X
              X     X     X     X
            ─────────────────────────
              1     1     3
              ─     ─     ─     1
              4     2     4
```

Use the data to answer the questions.

1. How many students are in the class?

    26

2. What is the range of the data?

   10

3. What is the answer that came up most often?

   3/4

4. How many students are at least half done? 22

   What fraction of the class is that? 3/4

Puzzler

Greene Farm has a total of 36 goats and geese. Farmer Greene reports that there are 100 legs in all.

How many of each animal are on the farm?

 20 geese

15 goats

5

Morning Jumpstarts: Math, Grade 4 © 2013 by Scholastic Teaching Resources

Name _____ Date _____

Number Place

Make a 4-digit decimal place value chart from tens to hundredths. Label the columns. Then write the following decimals in number form in your chart:

• fourteen and fifty-nine hundredths

• twenty and six hundredths

14.59

20, 6

FAST Math

Find each quotient.

720 ÷ 4 = _____   624 ÷ 3 = _____   2,900 ÷ 2 = _____

601 ÷ 7 = _____   1,024 ÷ 6 = _____   3,262 ÷ 5 = _____

Think Tank

Krin danced for 30 minutes every morning and for 45 minutes every afternoon for 5 days. How many hours and minutes did he dance in all?

6hrs and 15min

Show your work in the tank.

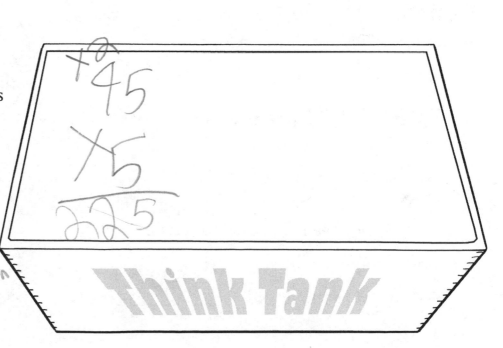

x2
45
x 5
225

Data Place

Use the data in the calendar to answer the questions.

APRIL

SUN	MON	TUE	WED	THU	FRI	SAT
			1	2	3	4
5	6	7	8	9	10	11
12	13	14	15	16	17	18
19	20	21	22	23	24	25
26	27	28	29	30		

1. Four dates in a row have a sum of 74. What are the dates?

   17, 18, 19, 20

2. Two dates in a row have a product of 240. What are the dates?

   24, 20

3. Which two dates have a quotient of 3 and a sum of 32? _____

4. Which two dates have product of 108 and a difference of 3? _____

Puzzler

When the power stops, so do the electric clocks. Solve the word problems.

1. The clock says 3:22 .

   The power has been back on for 7 minutes.

   It was off for 52 minutes.

   The correct time should be 4:21 .

2. This clock says 11:55 .

   The power has been back on since 11:45.

   It was off for 35 minutes.

   The correct time should be 12:30 .

80

Morning Jumpstarts: Math, Grade 4 © 2013 by Scholastic Teaching Resources

Name _____ Date _____

Number Place

Compare. Write **<**, **=**, or **>**.

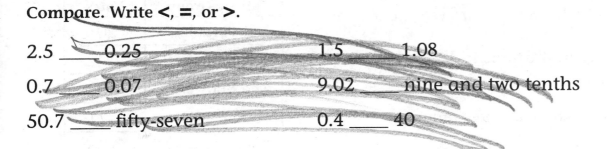

2.5 _____ 0.25   1.5 _____ 1.08

0.7 _____ 0.07   9.02 _____ nine and two tenths

50.7 _____ fifty-seven   0.4 _____ 40

FAST Math

Find each quotient.

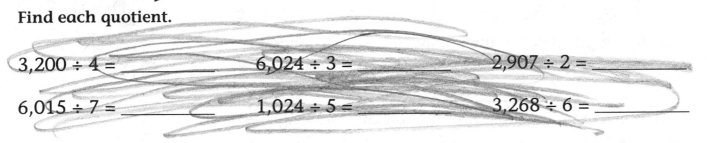

3,200 ÷ 4 = _____   6,024 ÷ 3 = _____   2,907 ÷ 2 = _____

6,015 ÷ 7 = _____   1,024 ÷ 5 = _____   3,268 ÷ 6 = _____

Think Tank

Greg does sit-ups every day. On 4 of the past 5 days he did 50, 60, 40, and 80 sit-ups. His average was 60 sit-ups a day over the 5 days. So how many sit-ups did he do on the fifth day?

_____

Show your work in the tank.

Data Place

All the students at Gershwin School were asked to name their favorite music group. The results for the top five answers are shown.

Use the data in the table to answer the questions.

Music Group	Votes
Hot Potatoes	203
The Mangoes	142
The Bugs	108
Louder Still	71
Popped Corn	36

1. How many votes did these groups get altogether? _____ 360

2. Which group got about $\frac{1}{4}$ of the votes?

   The bugs

3. Which group got $\frac{1}{3}$ the number of votes The Bugs got?

   popped corn

4. Which group got half as many votes as the Mangoes got?

   Louder still

Puzzler

Shade a picture in each grid. Draw anything you like—but make its area match the amounts shown.

0.34 + 0.3

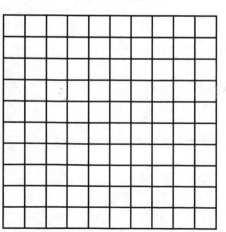

0.78 – 0.43

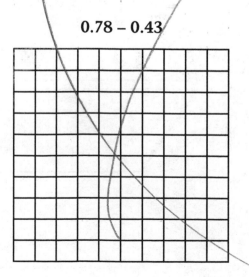

Name _____ Date _____

Number Place

Order the decimals from *least* to *greatest*.

0.42	0.09	0.35
0.63	0.2	0.43
0.4	0.04	0.38
0.75	0.57	0.06

0.09, .35, .42

.2, .43, .63

.04, .38, .4

.06, .57, .75

FAST Math

Write a fraction for the shaded part. Circle any fraction that shows less than one half.

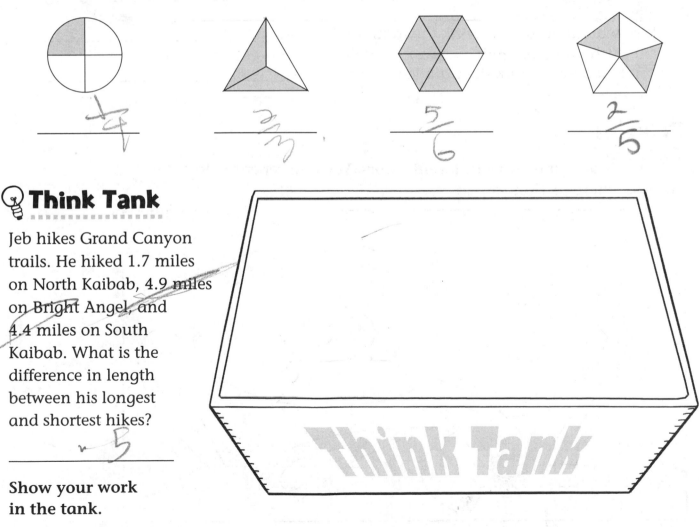

$\frac{1}{4}$ $\frac{2}{3}$ $\frac{5}{6}$ $\frac{2}{5}$

Think Tank

Jeb hikes Grand Canyon trails. He hiked 1.7 miles on North Kaibab, 4.9 miles on Bright Angel, and 4.4 miles on South Kaibab. What is the difference in length between his longest and shortest hikes?

_____ 5

Show your work in the tank.

Data Place

Use the train schedule to answer the questions below.

Leaves	Time	Arrives	Time
Tulip	10:00 A.M.	Rose	10:25 P.M.
Rose	10:29 A.M.	Lilac	10:44 P.M.
Lilac	10:48 A.M.	Crocus	11:26 P.M.
Crocus	11:30 A.M.	Aster	12:15 P.M.

~~Lilac~~ Rose

1. Which is the shortest trip? _____

Lilac

2. Which trip lasts 38 minutes? _____

2.

3. At what time do you think the train arrives at Tulip? _____

2.

4. When do you think the train leaves Aster? _____

Puzzler

Fill in this design using 4 different colors. You can repeat colors—
but not where sections touch.

Morning Jumpstarts: Math, Grade 4 © 2013 by Scholastic Teaching Resources

Name _____ Date _____

Number Place

Write the decimal from the balloon that fits
each clue. One number is *not* used.

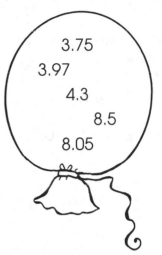

3.75
3.97
4.3
8.5
8.05

___8.05___ is much nearer to 8 than to 9.

___8.5___ is halfway between 8 and 9.

___3.75___ is the same as three and three fourths.

___3.97___ is a little less than 4.

FAST Math

Write a mixed number for the shaded area of each picture.

$2\frac{2}{3}$ $1\frac{1}{5}$ $3\frac{2}{4}$ $2\frac{1}{4}$

Think Tank

Renee spent $18.95 on a
scarf, $39.95 on sweater,
and $19.79 on a hat.
About how much change
should she get if she pays
with a $100 bill?

___21.31___

Show your work
in the tank.

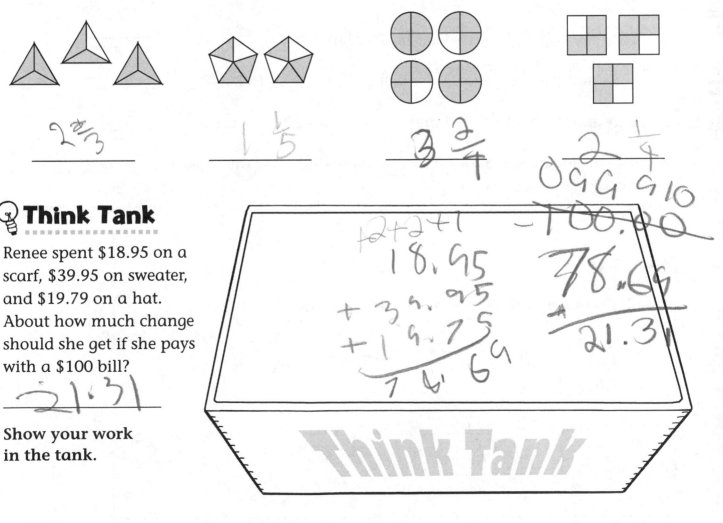

$$12+2+1$$
$$18.95$$
$$+39.95$$
$$+19.75$$
$$76.69$$

$$0\,9\,9\,9\,10$$
$$-100.00$$
$$78.69$$
$$21.31$$

Think Tank

Data Place

The line graph shows attendance at a new museum.

Use the graph to answer the questions.

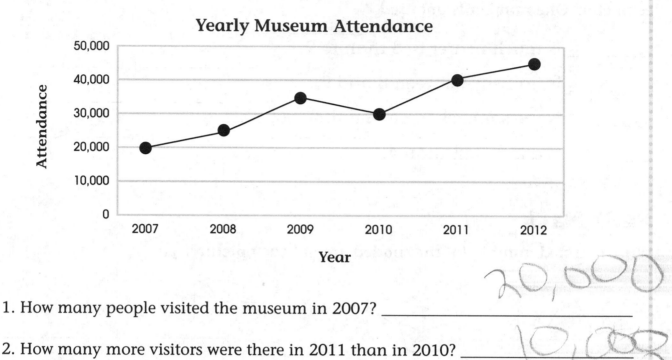

Yearly Museum Attendance

1. How many people visited the museum in 2007? _____ 20,000

2. How many more visitors were there in 2011 than in 2010? _____ 10,000

3. How many people visited the museum from 2010 to 2012? _____ 15,000

4. What can you say about museum attendance over the six years? _____ It
went ~~and~~ up and down

Puzzler

Write 2 times when the clock hands would form:

- a right angle _____ 12:15   9:00

- a 180° angle _____ 9:15   6:00

- an obtuse angle _____ 10:25   12:35

- an acute angle _____ 12:35
3:20
3:25

Morning Jumpstarts: Math, Grade 4 © 2013 by Scholastic Teaching Resources

JUMPSTART 40

Side A

Name _____ Date _____

Number Place

Order the decimals from *greatest* to *least*.

3.12	3.49	3.35	_____ 3.12, 3.35, 3.49
8.63	8.2	8.49	_____ 8.63, 8.49, 8.2
7.4	7.43	7.04	_____ 7.43, 7.4, 7.09
20.75	20.07	20.7	_____ 20.75, 20.7, 20.

FAST Math

Write each fraction as the sum of unit fractions.

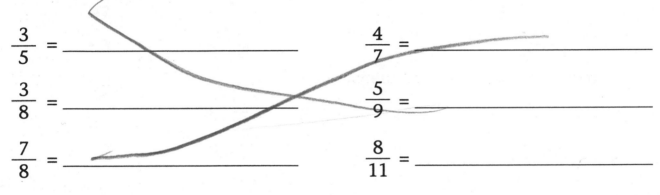

$\dfrac{3}{5}$ = _____

$\dfrac{3}{8}$ = _____

$\dfrac{7}{8}$ = _____

$\dfrac{4}{7}$ = _____

$\dfrac{5}{9}$ = _____

$\dfrac{8}{11}$ = _____

💡 Think Tank

Juan scored an average of 22 points per game for his first 12 games. He scored 18 points per game in the next 12 games. How many points did he score in the first dozen games he played?

_____264_____

Show your work in the tank.

$$\begin{array}{r} 22 \\ \times\ 12 \\ \hline 44 \\ +\ 220 \\ \hline 264 \end{array}$$

Think Tank

Morning Jumpstarts: Math, Grade 4 • © 2013 by Scholastic Teaching Resources

87

Data Place

Use the table below to tally all vowels in the riddle and in its answer.

Why is a giraffe's neck so long?

Because its head is so far from its body!

Vowel	Tally	Number
a	卌 卌	5
e	卌 卌	5
i	卌 卌	5
o	卌 卌	5
u	/	1
y	/	1

Puzzler

Write the weights you would use.

1 kg $\frac{1}{2}$ kg   750 g   50 g   225 g

Total Weight	Weights Used
975 grams	
1,800 grams	
2,300 grams	

88

Morning Jumpstarts: Math, Grade 4 © 2013 by Scholastic Teaching Resources

Name _____ Date _____

Number Place

Round each decimal to the nearest tenth *and* hundredth.

Number	Nearest tenth	Nearest hundredth
6.177	6.200	6.180
1.852	2.000	1.900
4.335	4.000	4.300

FAST Math

Write the value of *n* to complete the equivalent fraction.

$\frac{1}{2} = \frac{n}{6}$ _____ $\frac{1}{4} = \frac{n}{8}$ _____ $\frac{2}{5} = \frac{n}{10}$ _____ $\frac{3}{8} = \frac{n}{16}$ _____

$\frac{4}{8} = \frac{n}{4}$ _____ $\frac{2}{3} = \frac{n}{6}$ _____ $\frac{6}{10} = \frac{n}{5}$ _____ $\frac{5}{6} = \frac{n}{12}$ _____

$\frac{3}{9} = \frac{n}{3}$ _____ $\frac{3}{4} = \frac{n}{8}$ _____ $\frac{3}{4} = \frac{n}{12}$ _____ $\frac{7}{8} = \frac{n}{24}$ _____

Think Tank

Look at the fruit market signs.

Which market has the better buy on pears?

___apples___

How much better?

___4¢___

Show your work in the tank.

Fred's Fruit Market
Pears . . . . 3 for $.96
Apples . . . . 4 for $1

Fran's Fruit Market
Pears . . . . 6 for $1.80
Apples . . . . 2 for $.45

Think Tank

Data Place

Li tallied the kinds of vehicles that passed her house for 1 hour. Show her results in a line plot. Give the line plot a title.

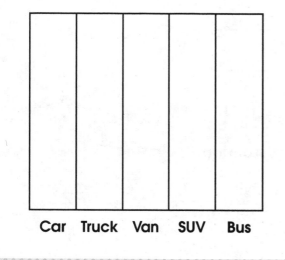

Car   Truck   Van   SUV   Bus

Vehicle	Tally
Car	|||| ||||
Truck	||
Van	||||
SUV	||||	
Bus	||

Summarize what the line plot shows.

_____

_____

_____

Puzzler

Use the fractions below to label the coins in each box.
Then find each total value.

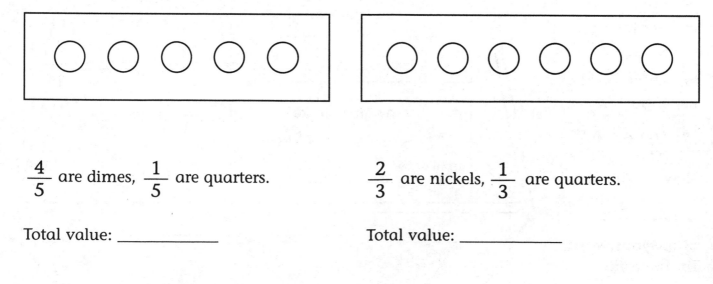

$\dfrac{4}{5}$ are dimes, $\dfrac{1}{5}$ are quarters.

Total value: _____

$\dfrac{2}{3}$ are nickels, $\dfrac{1}{3}$ are quarters.

Total value: _____

Morning Jumpstarts: Math, Grade 4 © 2013 by Scholastic Teaching Resources

Name _____ Date _____

Number Place

Write a decimal equal to each fraction.

$\frac{2}{5}$ _____ $\frac{2}{8}$ _____ $1\frac{1}{2}$ _____

$3\frac{9}{10}$ _____ $2\frac{6}{8}$ _____ $1\frac{3}{4}$ _____

$7\frac{1}{4}$ _____ $\frac{7}{10}$ _____ $5\frac{4}{5}$ _____

FAST Math

Find the sum or difference in simplest form.

$\frac{7}{8} - \frac{3}{8} =$ _____ $\frac{9}{12} - \frac{5}{12} =$ _____ $\frac{1}{7} + \frac{5}{7} =$ _____

$\frac{7}{10} - \frac{4}{10} =$ _____ $\frac{1}{9} + \frac{4}{9} =$ _____ $\frac{8}{11} - \frac{2}{11} =$ _____

$$\begin{array}{r} \frac{2}{6} \\ + \ \frac{4}{6} \\ \hline \end{array} \qquad \begin{array}{r} \frac{2}{5} \\ + \ \frac{4}{5} \\ \hline \end{array} \qquad \begin{array}{r} \frac{7}{8} \\ - \ \frac{2}{8} \\ \hline \end{array} \qquad \begin{array}{r} \frac{9}{10} \\ - \ \frac{7}{10} \\ \hline \end{array}$$

Think Tank

At 6:00 A.M. the temperature was 45°F. It rose 13°F by noon. What was the temperature at noon?

_____

Show your work in the tank.

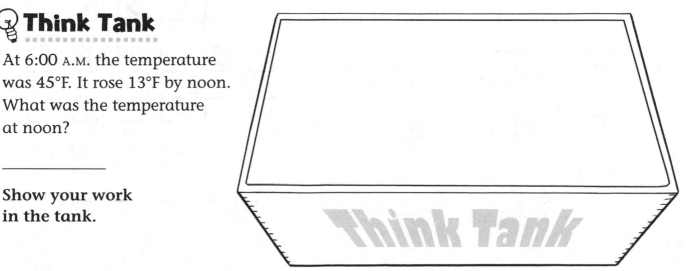

Data Place

Use the Venn diagram and numbers between 0 and 50. Write multiples of 4 in one part. Write multiples of 6 in the other part, and multiples of 4 and 6 in the overlapping part.

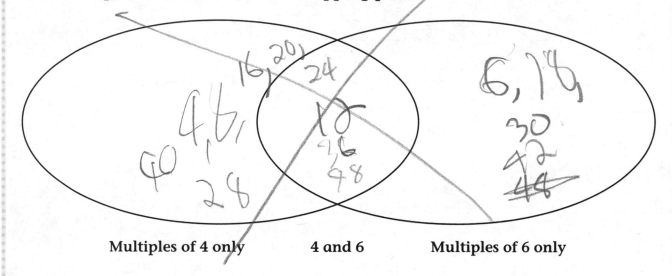

16, 20, 24
4, 6, 40, 28
16, 26, 48
6, 18, 30, 12, 44

Multiples of 4 only   4 and 6   Multiples of 6 only

Puzzler

Find each small array inside the big array on the right. When you find it, circle it and write its number.

1   2   3

Name _____ Date _____

Number Place

Write a fraction equal to each decimal.

0.35 _____   4.6 _____   3.75 _____   0.17 _____

5.97 _____   4.63 _____   0.85 _____   60.5 _____

FAST Math

Find the sum in simplest form.

$$6 \frac{2}{6}$$
$$+ \ 7 \frac{4}{6}$$
_____

$$4 \frac{2}{5}$$
$$+ \ 1 \frac{4}{5}$$
_____

$$3 \frac{1}{3}$$
$$+ \ 4 \frac{1}{3}$$
_____

$$1 \frac{3}{8}$$
$$+ \ 7 \frac{5}{8}$$
_____

$$6$$
$$+ \ 3 \frac{4}{9}$$
_____

$$2 \frac{2}{8}$$
$$+ \ 5 \frac{4}{8}$$
_____

$$3 \frac{1}{5}$$
$$+ \ 8 \frac{3}{5}$$
_____

$$2 \frac{2}{4}$$
$$+ \ 2 \frac{3}{4}$$
_____

Think Tank

Find the area of the figure.

Area = _____ square units

Show your work in the tank.

Morning Jumpstarts: Math, Grade 4 © 2013 by Scholastic Teaching Resources

Data Place

What if dogs could vote? The graph shows how 60 dogs might vote if asked what kind of food they'd like for dinner.

Use the graph to answer the questions.

Dinner Meal

Pizza Crust 12 | 24 Steak
12 Bone
9 | 3
Tuna
Liver Treats

1. How many dogs chose pizza crust? _D_

2. What food did $\frac{24}{60}$ of the dogs choose?
Steak

3. What food did 9 of the dogs choose?
Tuna

4. What fraction of dogs did *not* choose steak or tuna? _35/60_

5. Suppose 120 dogs voted. How many might a choose bone? _60_

Puzzler

Write a letter from the code to make each number sentence true.

A = 1	B = 2	C = 3	D = 4	E = 5	F = 6	G = 7
H = 8	I = 9	J = 10	K = 11	L = 12	M = 13	N = 14
O = 15	P = 16	Q = 17	R = 18	S = 19	T = 20	U = 21
V = 22	W = 23	X = 24	Y = 25	Z = 26		

1. $C \times \underline{H} = X$

2. $Y \div E = \underline{E}$

3. $Y - Q = F + \underline{B}$

4. $J + T = C \times \underline{}$

5. $\underline{J} - R = H \div A$

6. $U \div \underline{G} = C \times A$

7. $F \times \underline{L} = H \times I$

8. $C \times B + \underline{E} = K$

Morning Jumpstarts: Math, Grade 4 © 2013 by Scholastic Teaching Resources

Name _____ Date _____

Number Place

Write 3 decimals that belong between.

2 < _2.1 2.223_ < 3

12 < _12.1 12.212_ < 13

5.5 < _5.6 5.75_ < 6

9 > _9.1 9.2 9.3_ > 8

80 > _79.1 79.2 79.3_ > 79

3.2 > _3.11, 3.12 3.13_ > 3.1

FAST Math

Find the difference in simplest form.

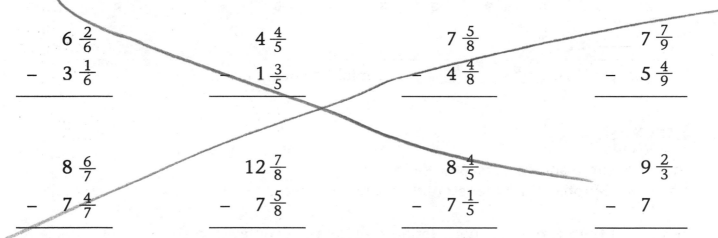

$$6 \frac{2}{6} - 3 \frac{1}{6}$$

$$4 \frac{4}{5} - 1 \frac{3}{5}$$

$$7 \frac{5}{8} - 4 \frac{4}{8}$$

$$7 \frac{7}{9} - 5 \frac{4}{9}$$

$$8 \frac{6}{7} - 7 \frac{4}{7}$$

$$12 \frac{7}{8} - 7 \frac{5}{8}$$

$$8 \frac{4}{5} - 7 \frac{1}{5}$$

$$9 \frac{2}{3} - 7$$

Think Tank

A tennis court is a rectangle 78 feet long and 27 feet wide. What is the area of a tennis court?

_____2106 feet_____

Show your work in the tank.

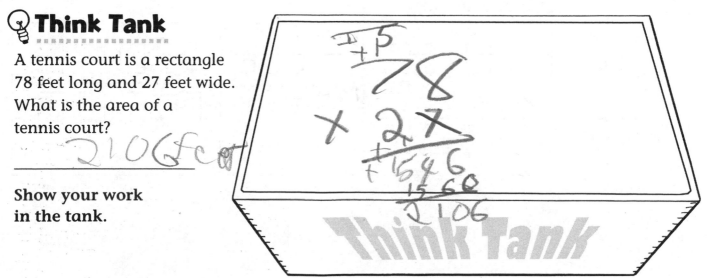

$$
\begin{array}{r}
78 \\
\times 27 \\
\hline
546 \\
1560 \\
\hline
2106
\end{array}
$$

Data Place

The chart shows five holidays in Mexico.

Use the data and your number sense to place and label each holiday on the timeline.

Constitution Day	February 5
Benito Juarez Birthday	March 19
Cinco de Mayo	May 5
Independence Day	September 16
Revolution Day	November 19

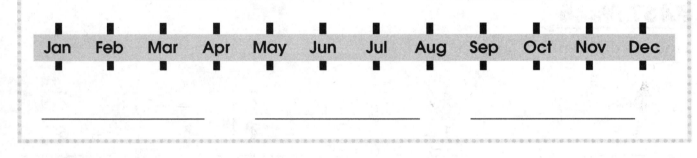

Jan   Feb   Mar   Apr   May   Jun   Jul   Aug   Sep   Oct   Nov   Dec

Puzzler

Each problem is shown in mostly letters.
Above each problem are the rest of the numbers it needs.

Figure out the number for each letter to make the problems work.

1, 2, 4, 6, 8		2, 3, 6	
N B Q × 6 ——— B, N W Q	☐ ☐ ☐ × ☐ ——— ☐ , ☐ ☐ ☐	C C C K ⟌ T T T	☐ ☐ ☐ ☐ ⟌ ☐ ☐ ☐

Name _____ Date _____

Number Place

Write 3 decimals that belong between.

$\frac{9}{10}$ > _____ > $\frac{5}{10}$ $\frac{2}{5}$ < _____ < $\frac{4}{5}$

12 < _____ < 12$\frac{1}{2}$ 8$\frac{1}{4}$ < _____ < 8$\frac{3}{4}$

5$\frac{1}{5}$ < _____ < 5$\frac{3}{5}$ 3$\frac{1}{4}$ < _____ < 3$\frac{1}{2}$

FAST Math

Find the product.

$\frac{1}{3}$ of 12 = _____ $\frac{1}{2}$ of 18 = _____ $\frac{1}{3}$ of 24 = _____

$\frac{1}{10}$ of 20 = _____ $\frac{1}{4}$ of 16 = _____ $\frac{1}{8}$ of 32 = _____

$\frac{1}{5}$ of 40 = _____ $\frac{1}{6}$ of 18 = _____ $\frac{1}{8}$ of 48 = _____

Think Tank

A book has 120 pages. One eighth of the pages have pictures. Two eighths have graphs. The rest of the book's pages have text only. What fraction of the book has neither pictures nor graphs?

_____

Show your work in the tank.

Data Place

The table shows scoring in the National Football League. The scoreboard shows the last time the Melons played the Pumpkins.

Use the clues to fill in the scoreboard.

Touchdown	6 points
Touchdown With Extra Point	7 points
Field Goal	3 points
Safety	2 points

Quarter	1	2	3	4	Final Score
Melons	3				
Pumpkins	2	3	6		

- The Melons scored a touchdown in the 2nd quarter.

- The Melons scored a touchdown with an extra point in the 3rd quarter.

- The Pumpkins scored a field goal in the fourth quarter.

- The Melons won the game by 4 points.

Puzzler

Use logic to figure out what a *nerp* is. Then solve.

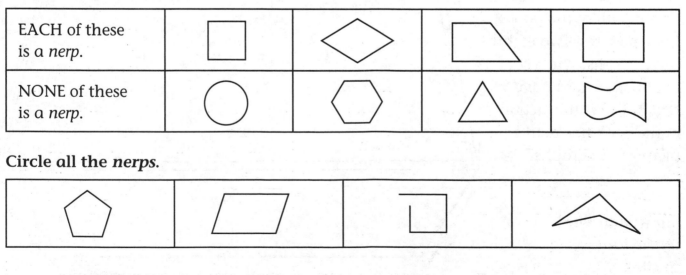

| EACH of these is a *nerp*. | | | | |

| NONE of these is a *nerp*. | | | | |

Circle all the *nerps*.

What is the rule for a *nerp*? _____

_____

Morning Jumpstarts: Math, Grade 4 © 2013 by Scholastic Teaching Resources

Side A

Name _____ Date _____

Number Place

Write the number that is *0.1* more.

2.2 _____   3.5 _____   7.8 _____

4.9 _____   6.61 _____   9.72 _____

Write the number that is *0.01* more.

3.23 _____   2.39 _____   9.06 _____

8.7 _____   54.09 _____   40 _____

FAST Math

Write each as an improper fraction.

$2\frac{2}{3}$ _____ $3\frac{1}{8}$ _____ $6\frac{1}{5}$ _____ $4\frac{3}{4}$ _____

$1\frac{7}{8}$ _____ $2\frac{5}{6}$ _____ $3\frac{4}{5}$ _____ $10\frac{1}{2}$ _____

Think Tank

Mori rode his bike $5\frac{3}{4}$ miles on Saturday and $4\frac{1}{4}$ miles on Sunday. Sam rode for $5\frac{1}{4}$ miles on each of those days. Who rode farther?

_____

By how much?

_____

Show your work in the tank.

Think Tank

Data Place

Use two dot cubes. Toss them 50 times. Make an X for each sum in the line plot below. Be sure you have 50 Xs in all.

What interesting things do you see in the data?

_____

_____

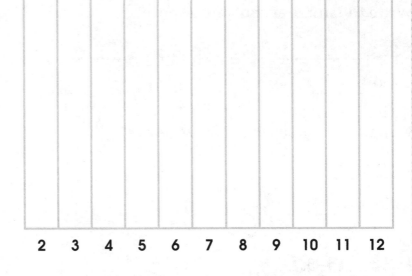

2   3   4   5   6   7   8   9   10   11   12

Puzzler

Solve each division problem. Then color.

RED   if the remainder is even.

YELLOW   if the remainder is odd.

BLUE   if there is no remainder.

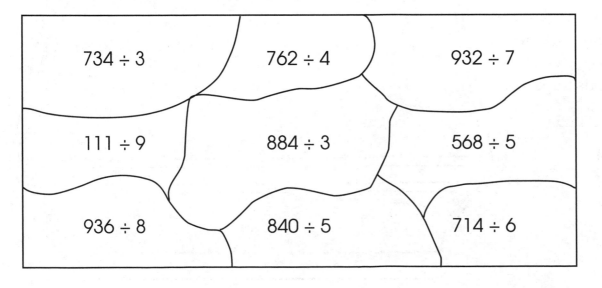

734 ÷ 3	762 ÷ 4	932 ÷ 7
111 ÷ 9	884 ÷ 3	568 ÷ 5
936 ÷ 8	840 ÷ 5	714 ÷ 6

Name _____ Date _____

Number Place

Write each money amount as a fraction or mixed number.

$4.27 _____   five dollars and twenty-five cents _____

$34.85 _____   eighteen dollars and seven cents _____

$.49 _____ $15.05 _____

FAST Math

Write each as a mixed number.

$\frac{8}{3}$ _____ $\frac{9}{8}$ _____ $\frac{11}{5}$ _____ $\frac{6}{5}$ _____

$\frac{17}{8}$ _____ $\frac{25}{6}$ _____ $\frac{24}{5}$ _____ $\frac{12}{10}$ _____

Think Tank

There are 24 students in Suki's class. One-half gets a ride to school. One-half of those comes by bus. How many students come by bus?

_____

Show your work in the tank.

Data Place

Ashley's Awful Foods is an awful place to eat. Check out today's lunch menu. Does it make you hungry?

Dirt and Onion Sandwich.	$4.75
Pebble Pancakes	$3.95
Acorn Omelet	$3.25
Rubber Band Burger . . .	$4.20
All Drinks	$1.00

Use the menu to answer the questions.

1. Dave orders pancakes and 1 drink. He pays with $10. What will his change be? _____

2. Omar orders the most expensive and least expensive foods. He has $10. Can he also buy a drink? _____ Explain. _____ _____

3. You have $15. You order 3 drinks. Can you order 3 burgers? _____ Explain. _____

4. Ella spent $5.95, including a tip of $1. She ordered a main course and a drink. What main course did she order? _____

Puzzler

A number cube has the numbers 1, 2, 3, 4, 5, and 6 on its faces. Here are two views of the same number cube. Answer the questions below.

View 1   View 2

What number is opposite the 2? _____

What number is opposite the 3? _____

What number is opposite the 6? _____

Morning Jumpstarts: Math, Grade 4 © 2013 by Scholastic Teaching Resources

Name _____ Date _____

Number Place

Compare. Write **<**, **=**, or **>**.

0.5 ____ $\frac{1}{5}$　　　　　0.2 ____ $\frac{1}{2}$　　　　　0.7 ____ $\frac{3}{4}$

0.65 ____ $\frac{65}{100}$　　　　$\frac{1}{2}$ ____ 0.2　　　　　$\frac{1}{6}$ ____ 0.1

$\frac{1}{4}$ ____ 0.4　　　　　$\frac{3}{4}$ ____ 0.8　　　　　$\frac{9}{10}$ ____ 0.9

FAST Math →

Solve.

$\frac{1}{2}$ of 400 = _____　　　$\frac{1}{4}$ of 400 = _____　　　$\frac{1}{8}$ of 800 = _____

$\frac{1}{3}$ of 600 = _____　　　$\frac{1}{2}$ of 700 = _____　　　$\frac{1}{6}$ of 300 = _____

$\frac{1}{2}$ of 1,000 = _____　　$\frac{1}{2}$ of 5,000 = _____　　$\frac{1}{10}$ of 1,000 = _____

Think Tank

There are 32 students in Carl's class. One-eighth of them send 10 or more texts a day. How many text at least 10 times a day?

_____

Show your work in the tank.

Think Tank

Data Place

The table shows miles between some cities in the state of Washington.

• Follow *across* a row for one city.

• Follow *down* a column for another.

• The number where they meet is how many miles apart they are.

Use the data in the table to answer the questions.

	Colville	Olympia	Wenatchee	Yakima
Seattle	350	60	148	141
Spokane	71	319	169	201
Tacoma	362	28	160	153

1. Which city is farthest from Seattle? _____

2. Which two cities are 319 miles apart? _____

_____

3. Which city is nearly as far from Spokane as it is from Tacoma?

_____

Puzzler

Follow the directions.

• Draw a ★ in each pentagon.

• Write a Q in each quadrilateral.

• Write an H in each hexagon.

• Draw an octopus in each octagon.

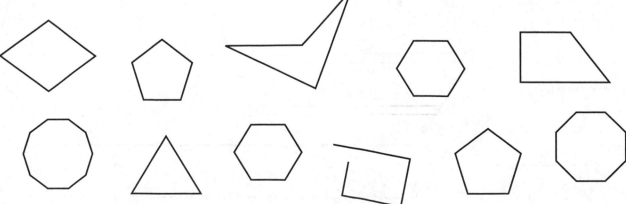

104

Morning Jumpstarts: Math, Grade 4 © 2013 by Scholastic Teaching Resources

JUMPSTART 49

Side A

Name _____ Date _____

Number Place

Compare. Write **<**, **=**, or **>**.

2.5 ____ $2\frac{1}{4}$ 1.25 ____ $1\frac{1}{4}$ 9.6 ____ $9\frac{1}{2}$

3.4 ____ $3\frac{3}{4}$ $8\frac{1}{2}$ ____ 8.2   3.7 ____ $3\frac{3}{4}$

3.9 ____ $3\frac{9}{10}$ $2\frac{1}{4}$ ____ 2.14   6.8 ____ $6\frac{3}{4}$

FAST Math

Find the answer. Watch the signs!

$$\begin{array}{r} 527 \\ \times\quad 6 \\ \hline \end{array}$$

$$4\overline{)981}$$

$$\begin{array}{r} 68,507 \\ -\ 7,819 \\ \hline \end{array}$$

$$\begin{array}{r} \$35.06 \\ +\ \$27.85 \\ \hline \end{array}$$

$$\begin{array}{r} 3.4 \\ +\quad 0.8 \\ \hline \end{array}$$

$$\begin{array}{r} 6.0 \\ -\quad 0.7 \\ \hline \end{array}$$

$$\begin{array}{r} \$4.61 \\ -\quad \$.88 \\ \hline \end{array}$$

$$6\overline{)624}$$

Think Tank

Which of the angles in the tank is an acute angle? Write its letter name.

_____

How did you know?

_____

_____

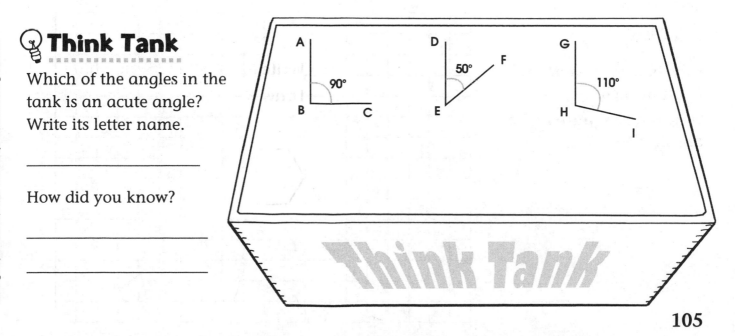

Data Place

The table shows stock market prices for three companies on one day. The decimals show prices in dollars.

Use the table to answer the questions below.

Company	Opening Price	High Price	Low Price	Closing Price
Dataworx	1.50	1.75	1.25	1.60
Healthco	8.15	8.80	8.15	8.75
Gametime	25.25	28.20	24.75	25.25

1. Which stock closed $.10 higher than it opened? _____

2. Which stock's high price was $.65 more than its opening price?

_____

3. Which stock's low price was the same as its opening price?

_____

4. Which stock had a difference of $3.45 between its lowest and highest price?

_____

Puzzler

Each box represents
1 square inch.

**How many square inches
are shaded?**

_____

Name _____ Date _____

Number Place

Read the clues to figure out the number.

• I am a 4-digit decimal between 10 and 20.
• My tenths digit is twice my tens digit.
• The sum of my tenths and ones digits equals my hundredths digit.
• The sum of all my digits is 11.

What number am I? _____

FAST Math

Multiply. Circle the pair of products that have a sum of 5,100.

| 33 | 23 | 42 | 48 |
| × 22 | × 11 | × 12 | × 99 |

| 64 | 75 | 62 | 44 |
| × 39 | × 29 | × 42 | × 83 |

Think Tank

I am a quadrilateral. All my sides are the same length. But none of my angles are right angles. Draw me in the tank. What am I called?

_____

Show your thinking in the tank.

Think Tank

Data Place

The chart shows how Shakir exercises for an hour each day.

Show the data in the circle graph.

Outline, shade, and label each section with the exercise it stands for.

Write the number of minutes.

Exercise	Parts of an Hour
Sit-ups	$\frac{1}{12}$
Stretches	$\frac{1}{6}$
Treadmill	$\frac{8}{12}$
Weights	$\frac{1}{12}$

Exercises in One Hour

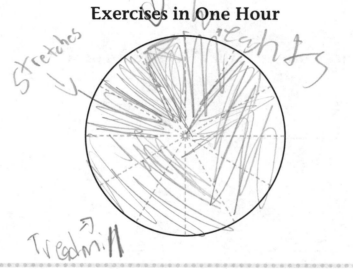

Puzzler

Half a bat appears on one side of a line of symmetry.

Shade in the rest of the bat.

Keep it symmetric.